CONTENTS

"It is the shots you don't play that are as valuable
as those you do."

George Dobell

COMPLEAT CRICKET

eight days in September

an account of the Division One

relegation battle in the

County Championship 2017

by Tim Cawkwell

Sforzinda Books, Norwich, UK, 2018

ACKNOWLEDGEMENTS

Highlights of all the matches described are available to watch on YouTube and include some remarkable wickets, whether bowled or caught. In the YouTube search bar enter the names of the counties in question and the year 2017. I am grateful to the journalists both in the print media and online who write so well about county cricket, and also to the commentators on local radio who manifest such pleasure in the game and knowledge of its myriad details. On 13 March 2018, just as this book was going to press, I learnt of the death on the day before of one such commentator, Dave Callaghan, a Yorkshire stalwart. He was aged 63 - may he rest in peace.

Except for the computer screenshots, including the lovely picture of the ground at Taunton on page 65, all photographs have been taken by the author.

PROLOGUE

No wonder English cricket's County Championship is a minority event. In an age of soundbites, video clips, eye-blinks, it takes hours not seconds. What is more it happens mostly on weekdays when most people are at work or at school. Why bother with it at all? The ineluctable answer is that it provides the seed-bed without which Test cricket in England would not survive. Cut out cricket's heart, stop the flow of blood, and the limbs would cease to function. It has to stay. So, how do you make it a spectator sport? One way is to provide an enthralling conclusion to the season. I began to get engaged with county cricket in 2015 with the Middlesex v Yorkshire match at the end of the season which produced an extraordinary game going from a seeming knock-out blow in the first over when Middlesex were no runs for three wickets, to the end of the match when they won (see my 'Cricket's Pure Pleasure'). 2016 was even better, when the last day of the season had Middlesex, Somerset and Yorkshire in a three-way tussle for the title, resolved at 5:30 PM on that day when Middlesex beat Yorkshire in dramatic fashion and seized the title (see my 'Tale of Two Terriers').

I had witnessed the 2015 conclusion by spending four days at Lord's. By 2016 I had got inside the mechanisms of the internet and followed events closely online, even from Italy where I was staying when the last day took place. Those experiences posed the question of what to do in 2017. I had the choice of going to watch a final game in real time, and the prospect of Somerset versus Middlesex in Taunton looked enticing, although I could not envisage how enticing it would prove to be. The alternative was to follow the games involving all sides online, via online ball-by-ball commentary, local-radio commentary, and as I discovered live streaming of matches. The first choice seemed to beckon on the grounds that cricket needed to be engaged with face-to-face. Yet there was a powerful reason to adopt the second method since it would allow me to follow the fortunes of all the teams involved and experience all the vicissitudes in real time. So I decided to watch it the way God would have. On the other hand, at the back of my mind there is a nagging and disturbing doubt about this new technology that allows us to engage close-up in things that are far away. Want to spy on the house where someone lives? Go to Google Maps. Want to find out what someone looks like? Try Facebook. Want to fire a missile at a hostile? Use a computer-controlled drone. None of those unsettling technologies can be undone, but I cling to their benefits nonetheless. For one thing, they allow us to be involved in following sport from afar. What is more, cricket is very well adapted for engaging with it in this way, since it affords time for online commentary, reflection, questions and replies, and punctuates that time with sharp moments of explosive action. Even a dot ball can fascinate us. A compromise was in order. I could book into watching Surrey v Somerset at The Oval on Day Two but spend the other days at home. I could decide what to do in the second week nearer the time.

What was at stake? Not on this occasion the contest for the title, but something scrappy, even more like arm-wrestling than normal, the contest between five teams to avoid the relegation spot. Four teams would be winners of a kind, but the loser would be consigned to humiliation of a kind.

*

I was 69 when I saw all that I did in 2017, and count myself fortunate that I had the leisure capacity to follow events. I ensured the diary was clear in advance, easily shifting a dental appointment unhelpfully fixed for Day Eight, that is to say Day Four of the second week. I had a sense at the outset that it would get in the way.

This following from afar seems especially important in assessing the popularity of county cricket. A rump of spectators attends matches at the grounds, sociable and well informed, in particular about the teams they support, but it is clear that many keep in touch from afar, apparently atomized but in fact much more linked up through social media than is initially apparent. The numbers are difficult to assess, but it is to be hoped that in all their radical deliberations about upheaving the cricketing order, the ECB have done research in this area. True, this support is barely monetised, if at all, which may render it of no account to some administrators. But there needs to be a wider understanding of its value as well.

Before describing the blow-by-blow events on those eight days, I conceived a flight of fancy on the lines of Izaak Walton's 'The Compleat Angler' with its long, and rather one-sided, conversations between Piscator (Fisherman) and Venator (Huntsman). Hence this Waltonian feature, a letter to the reader, 'especially to the honest angler'. For angler read cricket-lover.

LETTER TO THE READER

Dear Reader,

I must tell you about a most curious conversation I had in December 2016 while I was on my way to watch Test cricket in Mumbai by plane from London, not curious in itself because you have to pass the time and conversation is a way of doing it. However, it was with a complete stranger. This <u>was</u> curious since I am not one to start a conversation with someone I don't know, although I am happy enough to respond warmly to an invitation to converse from someone else.

I had been reading in a stop-start sort of way, but had come to a stop and was gazing blankly down the plane, when a voice broke in, "I could never imagine myself reading a book on that thing." Funnily enough, I was almost ready for this, having had this conversation a number of times already.

"What, on a Kindle? It's not difficult, you know. A page, some words, your eyes and your brain. One person told me they like a book in the hand because you could smell it and feel it. I did demur politely, but I didn't think much of the argument." I stopped there with a grin on my face, and he began laughing as if he took pleasure from the eloquence of my defence instead of offence at my sarcasm. That made me even more pleased with myself, and I was prompted to go further: "I could not help noticing you doing a lot of texting on your phone. Is there a difference between that and reading on a Kindle?"

"But that was business."

"And mine was pleasure." It flashed through my mind that a conversation could be conceived in terms of a cricketing duel, one player keen to score, the other keen for a wicket. As a bowler, I had to find out his weaknesses if I was to win the argument.

"What is the business if I may ask?"

He told me it was to do with textiles and then added, "I'm an Indian rising and shining, you could say."

I thought he had style but I felt a desire to probe his technique. "I've got the Upanishads on my Kindle, you know." This certainly caught him on the crease, uncertain whether to play forward or back. Yet he played it well enough, cheerfully admitting that they had passed him by.

I was walking back to my mark when he asked, "Is that what you were reading just now?"

"Not quite. Actually, I've got them on the Kindle, so I'm carrying them around everywhere, but I've hardly looked at them. I'd start and then stop. No, I was reading The Compleat Angler by Izaak Walton."

"Never heard of it, I must say."

"Why should you have? Walton was an English writer, seventeenth century. It's a book about fishing, but also in praise of the rural life. Pastoral, if you know what I mean. Complete is spelt C-O-M-P-L-E-A-T."

He clearly felt this bowling was too intense, and wanted to get down the other end since he then asked why I was going to India. I told him it was to watch cricket, which prompted him to feel he could deal with my bowling after all. He punched me hard through the covers: "What! To watch India thrash England again?"

This was chastening. I dredged my brain for a suitable riposte and came up with a long hop. "It's not the winning, it's the taking part," I said.

"That's what you were told at school, I imagine. Isn't there a good English word for that, like 'Tosh!'" He confidently pressed home his advantage. "It's not what the British were saying when they were combing the world for money, I mean during the Empire."

I needed to stick to line and length, to reassert the virtues of attritional cricket. I asked him whether he liked the game.

"I can't stand Tests, which are so slow, so boring. I follow the IPL though." There was a pause as he removed and replaced his gloves. Time-wasting, I thought to myself, he is not as confident as he sounds.

Quite unexpectedly, he started sledging. "Can you take a joke?" he said with a grin.

Now it was me pausing the game as I said – slowly – "I think so."

"Well, the conquest of cricket by the IPL is one in the eye for you imperialists."

"Not me personally."

9

"Not you, I'm sure! But your great-grandfather's."

I sensed a flaw in his technique. "It wasn't all bad. If we hadn't been imperialists, India would never have known cricket."

His backward defence shot was scornful in its way. "I am sure we would have found out about it, without you taking over the country."

Personally I felt that the accuracy of the bowling was causing a mild discomfort which might be exploited. "Not necessarily. The truth is that Indians fell in love with the game thanks to the British. The whole subcontinent did."

He shaped to cut me to the boundary by insisting that what Indians really liked was T20 cricket. I was having none of it. "Blast cricket!?! Now is that real cricket, I ask you? You Indians have a genius for monumental batting, a genius for spin bowling. That genius can only be truly expressed in long-form cricket, slow cricket. Block cricket, I call it." I thought I'd follow up by bowling him a tricky slower ball if I could. "What team do you support?"

"The one making me the most money!"

"You mean betting? Do you mean to tell me that one half of your brain is calculating the odds, that's the cool half, while the other half, the hot half, is overriding it in willing your team to win? That doesn't sound sensible. So, what team do you support?"

"Pune. Rising Pune Supergiants."

My first idea was to say I had never heard of them, but that was not true. "I've heard of them. With a name like that, who hasn't? Have you heard of the T20 team where I come from? They're called the Super Norwich Hyperbolists."

He laughed. "With a name like that, how could I not?"

I realised that in his way he was getting the measure of my bowling, and what is more he cleverly adopted a different stance and our contest became, I have to confess, more blast than block.

"Seriously, there's no money in your kind of cricket!" he said. "Fewer and fewer people are watching it. The powers that be are just going to have to ditch it."

"Money is not everything. 'It's a vexation and creates a fear to die.'" I realised this was a bad ball but Walton was still banging about my head. Fortunately he didn't murder it as he should have done.

"But what do you mean, Mr... Look, what should I call you? I feel we know each other well enough by now. I'm Vikram."

"And I'm Izaak. No, no, that's wrong. It is John."

He laughed, perhaps in puzzlement more than merriment. "Now what was I thinking? Yes. John, why should people be afraid to die because they have money?"

"Because they can't take it with them."

"Who cares about that!?! Anyway, there's no merit in this tedious cricket if people don't want to follow it. But look at the crowds you get at those T20 games."

"Bash and bang games."

"Yes, bash and bang games. Nothing to be ashamed of."

"My point is that there is a sort of virtue in slow cricket that you don't find in blast cricket."

Could a pull through mid-wicket ever be said to be executed sarcastically? Vikram was sarcastic. "So, there is no virtue whatsoever in the speed, the skill, the brilliance, the excitement, the colour, the noise, the atmosphere at these bash events?"

"No. There may be point in them, but no virtue. 'Study to be quiet.' That's what Izaak said, a sort of oriental wisdom come to think of it. Watching slow cricket is like his gazing at the river: it looks placid but what secrets are there within it? Watching it you cultivate a large measure of hope and patience. What is more virtuous than quiet contemplation? See what Izaak says here: 'There is no life so happy as the life of a well-governed angler' – when he says angler, I mean a spectator at the County ground – 'for when the lawyer is swallowed up with business, and the statesman is preventing or contriving plots, then we sit on cowslip banks' – actually I'm not sure that the seats at cricket matches are cowslip banks – 'and possess ourselves in as much quietness as these silent silver streams, which we see glide so quietly by us.' That is eloquent. You're a businessman, aren't you, not a lawyer?"

"Yes, I love it."

"But you have to use law, don't you? And I imagine you're preventing and contriving plots too. You could compensate for those stresses by experiencing slow cricket."

"But I love the stresses. And I go and watch a cricket blast to feel the joy of those things. I'm not going to find that on the third day of a Test match grinding along with no end in sight."

"Vikram, you're missing the point. Is it dull for a game to go over five days and be finally resolved in the last session?"

"I agree with you! The end can be exciting but in T20 you can jump straight to that last hour you're going on about. And what is worse than a five-day game that peters out in a boring draw?"

Line and length, I told myself. "Of course not all games will produce a riveting end, whether in slow cricket or quick cricket. My fascination is as much with the preparations for that final session, and in the longer game that fascination is more drawn out. Will a wicket fall? Will Kohli get his hundred? How will he get his hundred?"

"With a bit of blast cricket, I imagine."

I had to smile. "You may be right there. Test cricket does feel more aggressive than it used to be. That may be to do with practising getting a galloping century in quick cricket."

"I'm right then."

I needed to recover my bowling poise. "No. Quick cricket is over with the swish of a bat. You need to plan a batsman's downfall, ball by ball. The way Flintoff got Ponting at Edgbaston in 2005." Vikram started looking out of the plane window but I had to finish the over. "He had just taken a wicket and had four balls to trap Ponting. Each ball was a challenge, cutting into him so he just survived LBW, then a catch just short of gully, then another LBW appeal, and with the last ball, cutting the ball late away from him so it took the edge. Out, caught behind. He even lulled Ponting by bowling a no ball before he finally got him. That was really clever. You had it all there: huge skill, massive tension, and then a stunning result. It would have been a victory for Ponting if he had survived the over, but it was a victory for Flintoff. Tension needs time to work its magic. In fact, time is of the essence of slow cricket. Or duration rather. You have to immerse yourself in time, find a different rhythm within yourself, adjust both body and mind to it, and thus learn to exist slowly. Slowness is an ingredient of happiness . . ." Since Vikram was still looking out the window, I let my purple passage peter out since I wondered if he was listening to me at all. Yet his defence was sharp, indeed more attack than defence.

"Come on, you get plenty of tension in a T20 run chase."

"But you don't get a build-up. If the Flintoff-Ponting battle had taken place in a T20 match, Ponting could have got free by mistiming a shot that brings him a fortuitous boundary. Or of course mistiming the shot and getting caught. How dull is that?"

"Not dull at all! It brings me to my feet cheering."

"Or groaning."

"Sometimes, that's true. But still out loud."

"But what would be the point? The noise would drown your groans, your cheers even."

"Oh, I love it, the trumpets, the fireworks, the explosions."

"But that sort of noise belongs to a football match, not a cricket match."

"The IPL is like football! It was inspired by your Premier League!"

"Well, the money was. I call it the eloquent symptom of the tabloidification of culture."

"'Tabloidification'? Ugh."

"Yes, ugh. It's meant to be vile."

"But it's also pompous, don't you think?"

I smiled ruefully, regretting I'd bowled that particular ball, and fell to ruminating. Should I bring up the subject of fielding, I wondered? The truth is that blast cricket has done an immense service to the game in the way it has ramped up the skill of fielding, and given regular field practice in the art of spectacular catching. Vikram had not mentioned this, perhaps was indifferent to the point, but I knew that the ill wind of quick cricket had brought gain as well as loss. Taking myself off was called for rather than bowling on a wicket that gave assistance only to the batsman. It was time to shake hands and call it a day. I said emolliently, "Walton's got another good phrase, 'Good company and good discourse are the very sinews of virtue.' I've enjoyed our conversation."

"I have too," said Vikram. "But you must admit, John, I'm right. The future is with quick cricket, loud cricket."

"God, I couldn't bear it."

"You're going to have to."

"Ah, a forthcoming victory for Indian soft power and I'm back in the pavilion with a pitiable set of bowling figures to my name."

He softened somewhat. "Who cares? This is just a game we are talking about. We are bigger than the game. Look, here's my card."

I studied it. The name leapt out, Vikram Blastathan. "You're pulling my leg, Vikram. If your name is Blastathan then my name is Blocksmith." We both had a loud laugh at this point. "I think you should spend some time at the Test Match with me, Vikram."

"Not a chance. It's all right for you. I expect you're retired. I've got a business to manage. But tell you what, you could join me at a T20 match. We could go up to Pune. That's not far in Indian terms."

"It used to be called Poona when we were in charge. It's probably full of history. I'd like to go there, I admit."

"Well then, it's a deal," and we shook hands.

I never did get to Pune to see a T20 game, and Vikram was clearly not going to come to the Test match. After I got back to England, having watched them lose to India by an innings and 36 runs, I felt somewhat melancholic. This probably derived from an undercurrent of feeling disturbing my equilibrium, that the divide between blast and block was not going to be bridged very easily, and that Vikram may have been right, the people on the block side were going to be left stranded and unrescueable.

Yet time plays its own tricks. That was December 2016. Nine months later, I was revelling in a blockfest as the County Championship came to a rolling boil.

T.G.C.

DAY ONE   Tuesday 19 September

One might expect the biggest factor in determining the outcome of the Championship to be the weather but is the fact that the weather now allows the cricket season to end so late in the year yet another indicator of a rise in global temperatures? Despite this there was a distinct possibility that rain or bad light would come at an awkward time to disrupt proceedings and possibly influence them decisively. But things at least started well, with a dry albeit windy day forecast across England, or at any rate in London, Southampton and Leeds where the cricket was to be played.

Alertness was particularly required in appreciating where each team lay in the table, what points they had, and what points they needed. Essex (209 points) had the championship in the bag and at the other end Warwickshire (74 points) faced the drop whatever happened. Lancashire (153 points) were safe from relegation, so this left five teams truly motivated not just to win matches but to get bowling and batting points as well: Surrey (136), Hampshire (135), Yorkshire (124), Somerset (123) and Middlesex (123). As Scyld Berry remarked in *The Daily Telegraph* on 18 September, "Never has the County Championship been so cut-throat." Division One consists of eight teams, so if two are to be relegated, that is one quarter of the teams. The churn of teams ascending and descending the ladder is unavoidable, yet nevertheless welcome, certainly to the non-partisan spectator. For the committed, pleasure and pain were in store, agony for one set of supporters while relief, perhaps even an active pleasure in experiencing it, awaited the rest. As Berry remarked, "A bit of intensity in the final fortnight will not come amiss."

And a late-September fortnight of cricket it was, not the England-Windies bash, first of a T20 match and then five one-day internationals, but two rounds of four-day games scheduled for Tuesday 19 to Friday 22 September, then Monday 25 to Thursday 28 September. Two rounds of Championship matches were better than one, making it a game of two halves. Also there would be a weekend in between to absorb what had happened, to practice a kind of cricketing *dégustation*: what aromas would the results of the first round give off, what fruity flavours for the taste buds to savour – and what sournesses? 'If onlys' would occur, but the hope was that barely anything would have been resolved, turning the last round into the grandest of climaxes.

*

That Tuesday morning I got involved by looking at the newspapers online: *Times, Daily Telegraph, Guardian*. *The Guardian* had a perky blog from the lively Will Macpherson at Lord's, but, not unreasonably, the papers were leading on the prospects for the ODI series against the West Indies, the first being on Tuesday at Old Trafford. The T20 game at Durham on Saturday, the result of which is somewhere in the ether, was marked by the collapse of a temporary stand. It flitted facetiously through my mind that this was caused by the shockwaves of bat on ball and the high decibel levels caused by general razzmatazz. These were quibbles as it transpired: the game had been a sell-out.

I spent time studying the Championship points table and trying to permutate the effects of different results. At 10:30 it read as follows:

Essex   209 points   8 won, none lost, four drawn
Lancashire   153   four, two and six
Surrey   136   one, one and ten
Hampshire   135   three, two and seven
Yorkshire   124   three, four and five
Somerset   123   three, five and four
Middlesex   123   two, three and seven
Warwickshire 74   one, eight and three.

I eschewed predictions, except to note that Somerset had the hardest fight on its hands to escape being the likeliest candidate for the drop zone at the end of the week. But all this took time and having got distracted by the BBC live feed being devoted to the ODI, I only logged into ESPNCricinfo 20 minutes after the start of play. There the games were lined up on a menu bar at the top, so I had to ponder carefully the question of which of the four matches to follow: Hampshire v Essex, Middlesex v Lancashire, Surrey v Somerset, Yorkshire v Warwickshire, although the eye was drawn particularly to how Middlesex, champions in 2016, and Yorkshire, champions in 2015, would fare. In fact I found I did not have to choose because scores in all four games could be accessed at any time, although as I learned during the day, the pace of events became so frenetic it was hard to keep up with four games at once, and like in blast cricket the hyperactivity made you lose concentration in appreciating the virtue of particular contests.

By 10:53, Hampshire and Middlesex had both lost a wicket, and 41 runs in total had been scored with Somerset, batting first against Surrey, going best. This was due to the first cricketing hero of the day, Marcus Trescothick, more easily named as Tresco, 41 years of age and wearing spectacles under the helmet, pinging boundaries at The Oval. In this case, the ground was important since Surrey's 136 points had been achieved as a result of ten draws, with only one win and one defeat. There were a decent lot of batting points in there: but then here was a chance for Somerset to get their 400 plus runs and then five valuable points. Tresco had it in mind. At 10:52 he drove straight down the pitch, a stroke immaculately conceived and executed, and stood back to admire his handiwork (below). His partner, Eddie Byrom (20 years old), started to run then he too paused to admire the stroke. Age and youth became a theme of a kind running through the unfolding soap opera.

My entertainment was not just confined to Cricinfo, since at 11:30 I tuned in to BBC local radio on my PC to get ball-by-ball commentary from Radio London for the two games at The Oval and Lord's, Radio Leeds for Headingley and Radio Solent for the Ageas

Bowl. 15 minutes later I began to study feeds on Twitter, revealing a desperate situation at Lord's. I had found out earlier that the ball was "going all over the shop" there, a results pitch definitely, not least because Middlesex had been dragged down the table by too many draws (seven, with two wins and three defeats). Twitter then laid out the Middlesex meltdown: at 10:45 0-1 (Compton); at 10:59 11-2 (Robson), at 11:07 25-3 (Eskinazi); at 11:15 28-4 (Malan).

One feature of following cricket online is the way comments can catch you offguard. At 11:46 a tweet told us Middlesex were 56-4 and Voges was six not out, accompanied by an offer to translate it from French. Out of curiosity I clicked this only to learn that the tweet could not be translated. So why suggest it in the first place? Answer: because the name 'Voges' was in the tweet, it was assumed it must be in French.

Funny peculiar, and annoying. But more common, and more enjoyable, were the funny ha-ha comments, such as appeared on the BBC website. This one was funny peculiar – and LOL funny: "Most disappointed to see that Ryan Sidebottom won't be bowling to Ryan Sidebottom." It might have happened: Yorkshire's veteran Ryan Sidebottom (762 first-class wickets) was not after all playing against Warwickshire because of a hamstring injury, but Warwickshire's Ryan Sidebottom, the overseas player from Australia, was, so the chance of the delicious confrontation was lost, hence the disappointment.

I mused on the cycle of life: as one cricketer departs, another arrives. Bowlers wreak havoc on their bodies, which makes the Yorkshire Sidebottom's longevity in the game all the more impressive. In September 2017 he was 39. Warwickshire's Sidebottom's career had led him from Australia to the Birmingham League following a series of hamstring problems and stress fractures, but, *mirabile dictu*, his frame was holding together. He had now played for Warwickshire since early August and was making his mark. At 28, provided injuries could be banished, he was only likely to enhance his status as a bowler.

On the Somerset Twitter feed, you could watch a clip of all Tresco's "beautiful boundaries", of which he scored 11 in reaching his 50, which when repeated and repeated made him into a perpetual-motion machine. This meant that at noon Somerset were 75-0 prompting the comment, "Did someone tarmac over The Oval in April?" Elsewhere

Warwickshire were 47-4, Middlesex 62-4 and Hampshire 85-2, giving ten wickets in the first 90 minutes of play. Already one prescient wag noted that Somerset v Middlesex at Taunton in the final round sounded "like a real humdinger".

By lunch, one could conclude that the cricketing excitement was at blast rather than block levels: 241 runs had been scored for 14 wickets, including that of Trescothick LBW Batty for 65. Yorkshire's six wickets against Warwickshire had given them two precious bowling points already.

Within minutes of play resuming after lunch, Middlesex had lost two more wickets, and a race seemed to be on between Warwickshire (65-6) and Middlesex (81-6) as to who would be all out first. Somehow the infection was spreading to Somerset, since the Surrey bowlers were producing magic on The Oval tarmac under a blue sky. Were Somerset batsmen succumbing to gremlins in the pitch or in the mind? Or was the tarmac more lethal than first described? At 1:38 Somerset were 105-4, Middlesex 89-7 and Hampshire 134-4. 18 minutes later Somerset were 122-5 while Yorkshire had reduced Warwickshire to 112-6. Then at Southampton Simon Harmer, Essex's remarkable overseas find from South Africa, came into the attack for the first time and immediately had Sean Ervine brilliantly picked up by Varun Chopra in the slips making Hampshire 144-5 (below).

In the non-celebrity universe of the County Championship a name like Harmer has no cachet, and yet his role had been crucial to Essex's performance in the season. The radio was waxing lyrical too about another unsung bowler, Rikki Clarke, who had now taken three

Somerset wickets in nine deliveries, and at 2:12 got his fifth when he knocked back not one of Trego's stumps but two (below).

At 2:21 the scores were as follows:

Somerset 145-6 (Clarke's bowling)

Middlesex 142-7 (a green top)

Warwickshire 141-6 (relegated so demotivated?).

Hampshire on the other hand were 170-5 making them almost respectable by comparison with the others. It was proving challenging to keep up: half an hour later 685 runs had been scored so far in the day for 27 wickets. If not flourishing however, batsmen were digging in. Ian Bell, who had had an indifferent season for Warwickshire, had made a half century, and the indomitable Toby Roland-Jones, hero of Middlesex's championship clincher against Yorkshire in 2016, was doing something to rescue Middlesex by scoring 50 off 58 balls and moving to a century partnership with Ollie Rayner.

Online commentary is potentially a dry affair; clips of the action helped to bring it alive. At 3:08 Liam Dawson of Hampshire seemed to be caught Foster bowled Porter. I thought at first that Foster had just casually stuck out his right hand to snaffle the catch, while remaining quite unhistrionic. So was it in fact LBW? No. Under further scrutiny, the ball barely troubled the top of off stump, but enough to remove a bail. Such mini-dramas were adding spice to the main course.

Batting points came into view, very desirable for a team scrabbling at the bottom. At 3:16 Middlesex were 200-8, giving them one valuable batting point, but Somerset were close behind and at 3:37 they got there: 202-7. Tom Bailey had now taken five wickets for Lancashire, and at 3:31 Rayner reached his 50, both personal milestones that aided the collective effort. However, at tea Middlesex were 233 all out, 17 runs short of batting point number two. Somerset at 206-7 were struggling against Surrey on the supposedly placid pitch, although Steve Davies had reached 51. Hampshire were 243-8 and Warwickshire 195-8 (Jeetan Patel 82 not out). That equated to 33 wickets in the day so far for 701 runs. Blast cricket, eat your heart out.

After tea, at 4:07 Hampshire got their second batting point and at Headingley, Patel was fired up enough to get to his century, but not fired up enough to go beyond it. He had reached 96 on the second ball of the over, got his hundred on the third, then was out LBW on the fourth.

At 4:13 Warwickshire were the second team to be all out, in their case for 219, of which Patel and Bell had scored 151. But a few minutes later at The Oval things were looking up for Somerset, now only 14 runs off a second batting point; the radio told us that the Somerset flag was at its full glory. At the Ageas Bowl Hampshire were 254-8 when Kyle Abbott was Porter's fourth wicket, caught in the slips by Chopra

(above). They were quickly all out on 254.

Somerset were now nine runs off a second point, Dominic Bess and Steve Davies having shared in a fifty partnership. While waiting for the second point to arrive, I learnt that LBW dismissals could, in certain erudite circles, be described as 'pretty JH', in honour of the noted English historian JH Plumb. Is this notion appallingly dated, like the County Championship in general? Plumb's name was resonant among historians six decades ago as a specialist in the eighteenth century, the oligarchic toff epoch, a period which despite its fascinations somehow had never been fashionable, and the name surviving as an *outré* piece of cricketing slang, poised for desuetude. But its resonance is an element of cricket glory: this is a game with a rich historical narrative to which rich footnotes have been added. Snapping back from this reverie, at 4:26 I learnt that Somerset were on 251 runs, and the second batting point had opened up a one-point gap over Middlesex who were now coming into focus as their main competitor in the struggle to avoid relegation. Since the final round was between these two teams, this prompted the sly question on the radio: are Somerset giving Middlesex a lift back to Taunton after the two games are over?

What is more Somerset had three wickets in hand: could they even get a third batting point with the Davies-Bess partnership trucking along? No, their nemesis that day, Rikki Clarke, having just got Bess for 27, at 4:57 had Davies caught on 86, his seventh wicket. Clarke's bowling had given the session to Surrey despite Somerset's resistance.

No sooner had this little drama reached its conclusion than I found another one shaping up at the Ageas bowl: mighty Essex, not having lost a Championship game all season, in their reply to Hampshire's 254 had gone from 1-1 to 12-2 to 12-3. Nor was there any let-up at Lord's, since at 5:13 Lancashire were 56-4 in reply to Middlesex's 233. So which team would emerge from this round with a victory: Middlesex or Somerset? With Middlesex's bowling attack (Roland-Jones, Finn, Murtagh, Rayner), surely they would beat Lancashire? Would Surrey succumb to Somerset's bowling attack (Craig Overton, Groenewald, Trego, Bess and Leach) on a pitch that was far from tarmac? Surrey had started their innings to find that every ball was an event, as the radio put it. At 5:48 they were 35-0 after ten overs and Trego, on in place of Overton, was starting to nip it about. Stoneman and Burns were surviving precariously, but they were surviving. The day was drawing to a close and the blue sky at The Oval meant the ground was being invaded by shadow. At 5:56 stumps had been drawn at Headingley with one intriguing event: I learnt that Kraigg Brathwaite, the West Indies batsman who had achieved cricketing immortality by steering the Windies in their fourth innings to a win at the Headingley Test against England with an imperturbable 95 runs, was now playing for Yorkshire – perhaps Headingley was now his favourite ground – and had been dismissed for 18. At 6:02 it was stumps at The Oval, Bess being denied a confident LBW appeal in the last over, so Surrey had negotiated 14 overs without loss. This was a platform for the next morning, when *The Times* verdict was that Somerset had bowled fractionally too short to find an edge, so they were going to have to bowl like demons, especially with the prospect of Sangakkara batting at number four. In Southampton a Hampshire performance was stunning the dozing champions with six wickets for 26 runs.

Only at 6:23 did play finish at Lord's with Lancashire on 113-5, advantage Middlesex were it not for the fact that Roland-Jones, squarely in line for a place in the England team to go to Australia that winter, had to trudge off before the end. It did not feel ominous. 'Lower back stiffness' was the official prognosis, and Adam Voges, the Middlesex captain, was sanguine enough that RoJo would be fine by the morning. The physios probably knew otherwise, and, although he did bat in the second innings (crisis being the mother of necessity), he bowled no more. Further he was then declared unfit for consideration for the Ashes squad. Truly the season takes its toll: he had bowled 277 overs for Middlesex in the Championship, and 134 overs for England in Test matches. This was not to overlook his crucial 102-run stand on the first day with Ollie Rayner spread over 21 overs.

At the end of Day One, the scores were as follows:

Hampshire	254 all out	v Essex	33-5
Warwickshire	219 all out	v Yorkshire	62-1
Middlesex	233 all out	v Lancashire	113-5
Somerset	269 all out	v Surrey	42-0.

Accumulating these figures, you get 1,245 runs for 51 wickets, equating to 24.4 runs per wicket. Thanks to real-time commentary online and on radio, I had enjoyed a riveting day, one (as *Guardian Live* put it) "bulging with wickets". Which result was the most surprising? Probably Essex's loss of five wickets for 33 runs was the hardest to predict. The Oval was a draw ground, until Clarke got into the Somerset batsmen. Lord's on the other hand was a results pitch: Middlesex needed a win not a draw, and did not want bad weather to deny them. Only the Yorkshire-Warwickshire match seemed to be as expected, but that did not explain Patel's century ("uncluttered by relegation" as David Hopps put it) nor Yorkshire conceding 142 between lunch and tea.

I ended the day smugly pleased that the next seven days of county cricket would be clear of all other engagements, but the second day was going to be different from the first, as I was booked to attend The Oval for some real cricket, not the virtual stuff.

The points table now read as follows:

Surrey   139
Hampshire 136
Yorkshire   127
Somerset   125
Middlesex   124.

Surrey felt safe to me, but technically they were not free of the drop. The other four teams however were far from safe.

DAY TWO   Wednesday 20 September

A 10:30 start at The Oval is too early for my train from Norwich, so I arrived at the ground after play had begun. I am always sorry not to see the first ball of the day, instead coming up the steps to be greeted by the sight of the game in full progress. A part of my brain feels dragged in a metaphysical direction, concluding that the play had been from everlasting to everlasting, a ghostly narrative that only takes on real form when my eyes record it. On the other hand another part of the brain knows that what is happening is solidly three-dimensional, especially faced with the keen question of where to sit.

I could not sit in the Members' pavilion, and the south west side of the ground was closed off making and imposing but empty bank of turquoise seats revealing an inscrutable set of initials painted on them: OCS. But there is all the north-east side seating as well as behind the bowler's arm at the Vauxhall End. Sun or shadow? Take your pick, Sir. We picked the Peter May stand.

My friend Steve and I went down to the front row, square on to the wicket, and I was reminded again – it happens each time I watch the first-class game – of the distance between the batsman and the wicket-keeper and slips. While on television slip-catching and wicket-keeping

look impossible, being foreshortened so they appear closer to the bat, the focus of real time makes it just about comprehensible.

By 11 a.m. I was firmly in my seat, I had caught up the news with Steve – what is the art of cricket without the art of conversation? – and had some coffee. Today I was off-line and it was a day for my camera. I got it working at 11:20 and happily clicked away until 5:15 when the exhausted battery told me, "no more," not unreasonably in view of the number of pictures I had taken.

It was definitely Surrey's day. They went from 42-0 to 328-6, 58 runs ahead of Somerset with four wickets in hand, and Sangakkara still at the crease. In the late afternoon a small group of Surrey supporters, suitably juiced by this time, began to sing, "You're going down," a football taunt directed towards Somerset which feels just not cricket. About the same time, Byrom saved a boundary but as he did so his feet possibly just touched the rope although no boundary was given. This prompted cries of "cheat" from the same group behind me. Again, it felt out of the spirit of cricket: how Byrom was meant to field it and be certain his feet touched the rope eluded me.

The sub-theme of youth and age was noticeable. The Somerset captain Tom Abell (23) consulted the elder statesman Trescothick on what to do - the photograph on the next page shows them plotting. Even more starkly two of Sangakkara's partners, Ollie Pope and Sam Curran (both 19), as they banged the Somerset bowlers to the boundary, went to King Kumar to bump fists, as if this connection would allow cricketing electricity to flow from the older to the younger.

Even more definitely than Surrey's day it was Sangakkara's day. He came to the crease at 12:14, with the score on 114-3, the key wicket for Somerset to take. As happened with six of the other teams in the Championship, it eluded them. Surrey were 150 after 52 overs, 200 after 12 more overs (64.2 overs), 250 after 11 more (75.4 overs), 300 after 16 more (91.3 overs). There was only a slight deceleration at the end of the day when Surrey felt that grinding Somerset down would suit them just fine.

At 5:15 Sangakkara hit a boundary to reach his century. My camera was poised to record the moment but the ball before, the battery died, and like the foolish virgin in the Bible I had no spare. Still, no image can match the bare recital of Sangakkara's contribution to Surrey's season. At the end of that day he had scored 1,369 runs in 13 innings at an average of 124.45 apiece. I had just witnessed his eighth century of the season in nine matches. Was it something about the pitch at The Oval? If it was one that Surrey exploited to their own advantage – for, besides Sangakkara, Burns and Stoneman both posted 1000 runs in first-class matches for the season – why did it not attract the opprobrium that the fizzing pitches at Taunton seemed to do? The answer was clear: all sides want good batsmen so theoretically they would all benefit at The Oval. There seems to be less enthusiasm for developing the art of spin, which was Somerset's speciality and one it exploited at Taunton.

In Somerset's first innings, the Somerset batsmen had started by scything the ball away, but when Clarke had come into the attack he had embarked on his own bout of scything, producing his best bowling figures in Championship matches, seven wickets for 55 runs. Somerset could have done with him, because even though Surrey had struggled at the end of Day One Somerset were unable to prevent them picking up the score and moving it forward.

It was puzzling that Tom Abell bowled himself so much. His figures on Day Two were 11-1-52-0, whereas before, in 43 first-class matches, he had bowled in only six innings: 17.4 overs, 58 runs, one wicket. At the end of the day these figures had become 28.4 overs, 110 runs, one wicket. This season, his first as captain, had been a test of character for him. Up to this match his scores had been 1, 0 / 1, 0 /8, 35* / 40, 5 / 6, 71* / 0, 4 / 0, 0 / (missed a game) / 96 / 30, 0 / 82, 51 / 46, 8*. He had got out for under ten runs twelve times. So, did he put himself on to bowl in order to lead from the front? At the beginning of September, in the game against Warwickshire he had resorted to oratory to motivate the troops and, no doubt, himself, with good results. Somerset won, and he scored 82 and 51. Could he inspire them, and himself, with his bowling? Or was there a more prosaic reason that one of his bowlers was suffering from a suppressed injury?

Of the Somerset bowlers, only Peter Trego was really on song, taking four wickets. The spin twins could not penetrate and in the whole innings, while Leach's nine overs only went for 25 runs, Bess's thirteen went for 65. It was no surprise that Leach's naturally furrowed brow seemed to suit his day,

and Bess looked markedly disgruntled at the end of it.

In the afternoon the sun screened by cloud caused the ground to look sombre,

and there were two brief departures for bad light. There was one bright spot for Somerset at the end of the day when Overton took a sharp catch to dismiss Curran, using his long limbs to snaffle the ball to his right - see next page.

*

Returning home, I learned that the real excitement had been at Lord's, and had a pang that I should have gone there instead of The Oval. A fool's game this: I would have missed King Kumar's masterclass.

In the Middlesex-Somerset contest, Middlesex seemed to be edging ahead: Lancashire had been bowled out for 165, 68 runs behind Middlesex's 233, but they had then been bowled out in turn for 152. At the close of play Lancashire were 46 for 1, needing 175 more runs to win. Would RoJo's absence be fatal for Middlesex? Although he had in fact batted, making nine runs, he had looked like "a man who had forgotten to take the hanger out of his shirt" as Vithusan Ehantarajah eloquently put it on Cricinfo.

The points table for the five in the frame now looked like this:

Surrey   142
Hampshire 140
Yorkshire   129
Somerset   127
Middlesex   127.

If each team in the strongest position were to win their game, the table would look like this:

Surrey   158
Hampshire 156
Yorkshire   145
Middlesex   143
Somerset   127.

So if Middlesex won their match and Somerset lost, then Taunton became the OK Corral.

There were other twists. If Yorkshire were to lose to Warwickshire, then they would be in trouble too. At the end of the day Warwickshire had been 219 all out, and Yorkshire were then bowled out for 296. Warwickshire were 49-1 in their second innings, still 28 runs behind. Yorkshire must have had confidence in a win but but they were going to be batting in the fourth innings, when Warwickshire would be well placed to apply bowling pressure.

The serious business of the County Championship: Tom Abell, Dominic Bess, Kumar Sangakkara.

Sangakkara poetic in defence

Ducking a bouncer . . .

. . . working to leg . . .

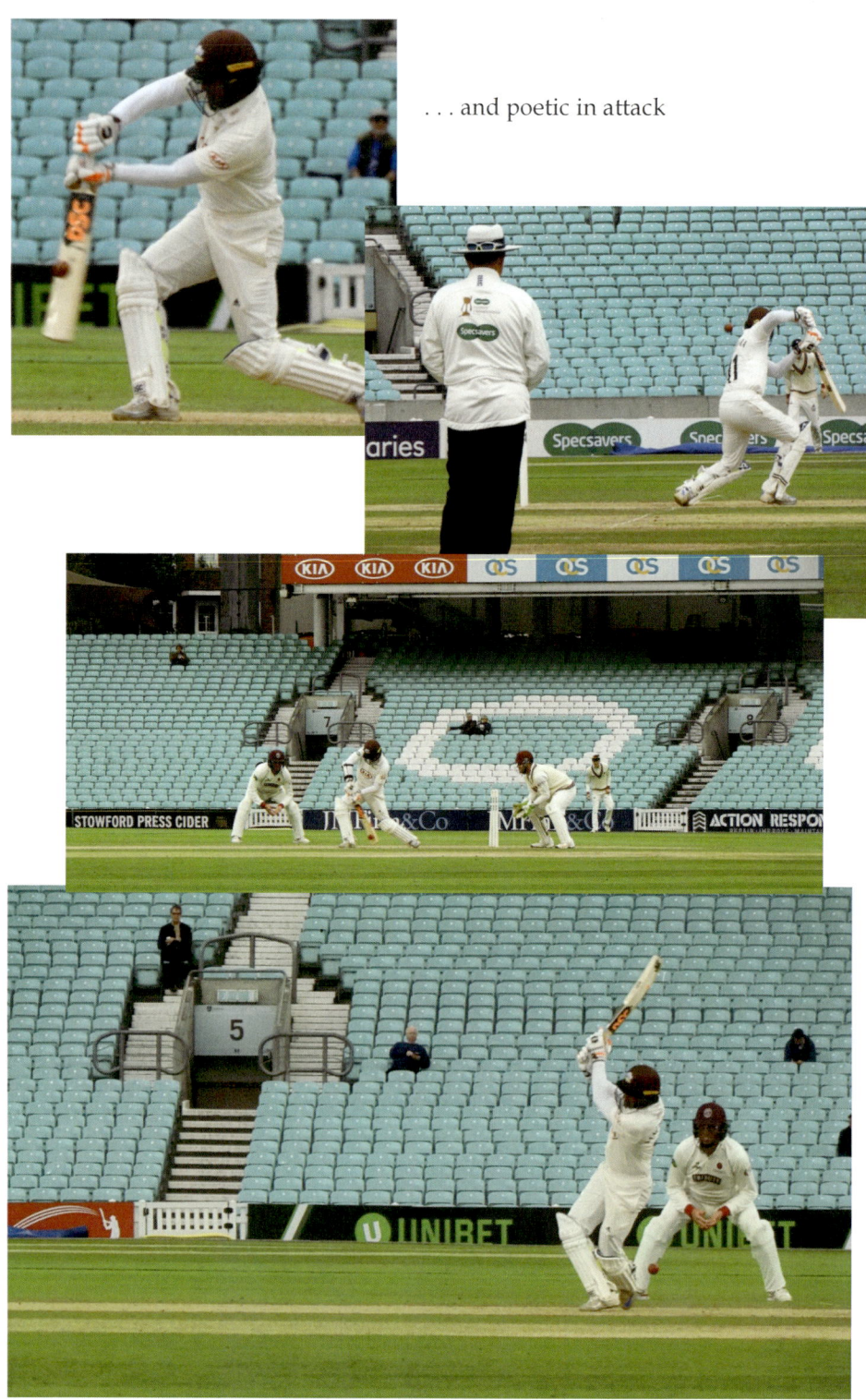

. . . and poetic in attack

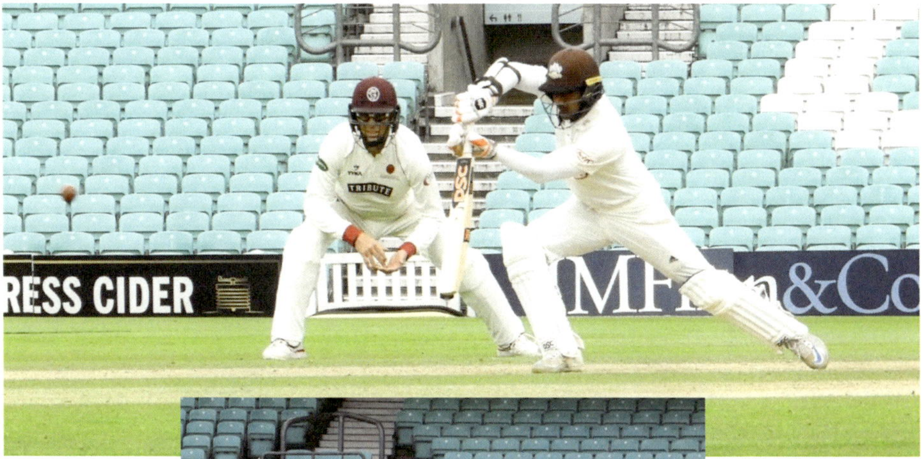

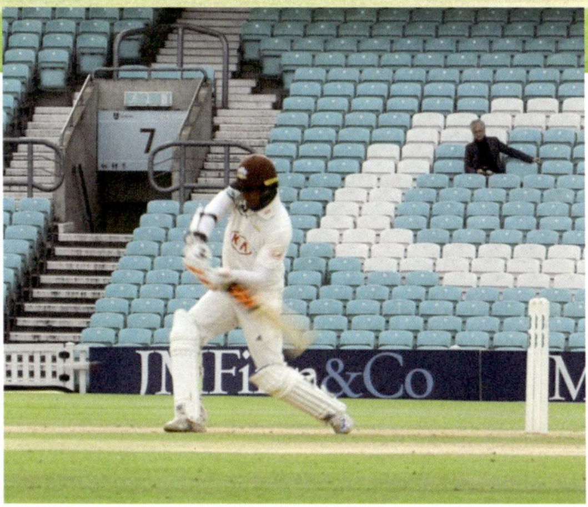

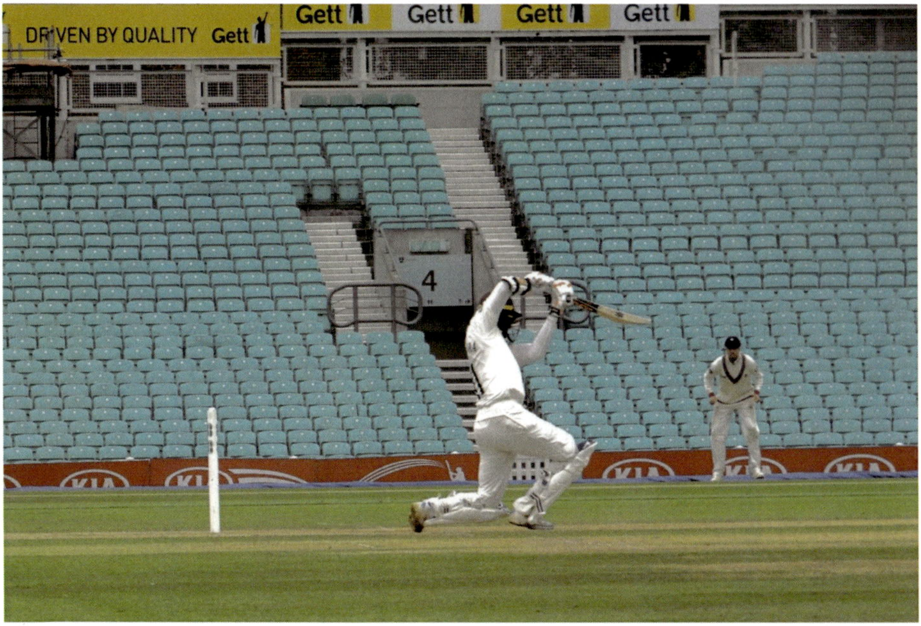

SANGAKKARA HITS BESS FOR SIX -
from the side and from behind the bowler's arm

Sangakkara cuts Overton for four to reach his century

DAY THREE   Thursday 21 September

Back at my desk watching on Cricinfo, the menu of scores in the bar at the top were: England v West Indies, India v Australia, Bangladesh v South Africa XI and, in the ICC WCL championship which in my parochialism had passed me by, Namibia v UAE. I admire cricket's global ambitions, but was focused instead on the antediluvian English county v English county set-up, this game of discarded thrones.

The choice was obvious: continue to follow either Surrey v Somerset and urge on Somerset's obduracy to earn a draw (or if not that, Sangakkara to get his double century), or Middlesex v Lancashire at Lord's and get bewitched by Middlesex's push for a crucial victory before going into the final round.

At 10:30 when the action fired up, I was following both games, listening to Middlesex v Lancashire on Radio London (and in view of the interest in the result Radio Five Live Sports Extra got in on the act as well), and following Surrey v Somerset on the ball-by-ball commentary. I did not have long to wait for something spectacular: at 10:45, Steven Finn sent Liam Livingstone's off stump cartwheeling.

Nine minutes later Steven Croft was LBW to Finn. Two good wickets for Middlesex. This was riveting but at 10:56 I found Surrey v Somerset on a live YouTube feed. The full screen gave a reasonable picture (720p HD) and for the first time in a long time I could watch live cricket free in my own home. Live cricket! Not highlights which for all the pleasure they give turn Test cricket into blast cricket. Even when they are watched in ignorance of the result, highlights still feel largely a sequence of fortuitous moments rather than events grounded in a long passage of play or sustained pressure from the batting or the bowling side. They destroy the sense of time which live cricket conveys so strongly.

However, there was one particular curiosity to contend with: the camera was fixed high behind the bowler's arm at both ends, without lateral movement and only a medium-shot view. If the ball went off the square you had to use your imagination to decide what was happening. This produced some intriguing moments during the day. What it revealed immediately was that Sangakkara was resuming his flow of runs. By way of example, the 110th over was scored as follows: dot, dot, four, dot, two, four, making ten off the over, all from his bat. At Lord's a similar veteran, Shiv Chanderpaul, was coming to the wicket at the age of 43 but then the sportive pitch at Lord's did for him: he was LBW to Murtagh and Lancashire were 59-4. This game was now the lead story on the BBC Sport website.

All this must have been disheartening to Somerset supporters, but their Twitter feed kept their spirits up by claiming that the "theme of playing and missing" was continuing at The Oval as the Somerset bowlers pressed for wickets, a judgement not confirmed by the YouTube feed. At 11:16, Bess was bowling into footmarks outside the left-handed Sangakkara's off stump: dot, two (inside edge), four, four (the King dances and the ball flies high to the offside boundary), dot, one – 11 for the over. At 11:24 Bess's line felt all wrong: Sangakkara took a single and then Clarke hit three more fours in the over. At 11:35 Surrey reached 401. They were turning the screw on Somerset.

If the Somerset team had been watching at Lord's, there was not much comfort to be had there. Lancashire's Haseeb Hameed was at the crease, battling for his team, and battling too for inclusion in the Ashes squad. Opening at number two, in the first hour of his innings he had made one run but having reached 23, made from some 60 balls, this hard-to-crack nut, more brazil than pea, that Middlesex had to wrench apart if it was to progress to victory, was hit on the hand. The game went into a coma as Hameed fought to stay at the crease by finding a comfortable way of holding the bat, but could not. The score was 75 and Middlesex still only had four wickets, but Hameed's retirement gave them momentum. At 11:45 Voges no doubt wishing to give Finn a rest replaced one tall bowler with another by introducing Rayner's spin, Rayner being 6ft 5in to Finn's 6ft 7in. At 11:47 Dane Vilas reverse-swept for a boundary, taking him to 20, and then clipped a second, making Lancashire's target 136 with wickets in hand, eminently achievable even with Hameed sidelined.

At The Oval Abell had put himself back on. Having hit Sangakkara on the pad he appealed for the LBW to no avail, but then something visually very curious happened: Sangakkara hit Abell very high, and while the camera remained fixed on the pitch (below), I assumed it had sailed over the boundary. In truth it was a 'time to get out' shot which judging by the bowler's glum expression had gone for a boundary. In fact the catch was held in the deep by Leach. There was something sensible in Abell not getting excited.

Somerset continued to strive: Abell went past the edge of Gareth Batty's bat, and Trego was swinging it into the right-hander. At 12:08 (Lord's) Finn had gone for two boundaries, and Lancashire only needed 107 runs. At 12:10 (Oval), with Surrey on 425-7, Batty cross-batted Abell to leg, looked to set off and then decided against it. The non-striker Clarke was caught well out of his crease and George Bart-lett's direct throw at the stumps, off screen of course, both hit them and caught a pigeon by surprise.

This little bit of drama was captured in a six-second clip on the Somer-set Twitter feed, and could be watched repeatedly in a version of cine-matic minimalism. Surrey were now 425-8. Somerset continued to fight but even a draw was beginning to look a challenge unless the weather was going to play a part. At Lord's at 12:17, Middlesex made their breakthrough when Vilas was caught at the wicket off Finn for 37 runs, making Lancashire 116-5, Vilas 20 or 30 runs short of what was needed from him, and Lancashire still 105 runs adrift of victory.

Somerset were cleaning up the Surrey tail when the YouTube feed froze without explanation except for a cheerful "Thanks for tuning in". Crestfallen, I fell back on the online commentary for an over or two until spirits were re-animated by Trego sending Meaker's stump flying on Twitter (below). Surrey were all out for 433.

Although attention had to switch back to Lord's, I got a breather since lunch came soon with Lancashire on 135, needing another 86 runs with five wickets remaining, including that of the injured Hameed. Considering they were without Roland-Jones, Middlesex had done particularly well, thanks especially to Finn who had four of those five wickets. At The Oval, Somerset had a day and a half to bat out if they were to get a draw, but went into lunch one wicket down, Tresco having been caught in the slips for one run.

In fact, the two other matches were not without their intrigue. Hampshire had knocked Essex over for 76 and made them follow on only for Essex to pull themselves together and get to 226 for the loss of three wickets. At Headingley Warwickshire (219 and 136-3) led Yorkshire (296) by 59 runs with seven wickets remaining. So Essex and Warwickshire to win I wondered?

*

After lunch at Lord's, the tension mounted, as a four off Finn brought Jordan Clark to 29 and Lancashire to 150, needing 75 to win. Here was the essence of slow cricket's pleasure: the winner would be the team not with the greatest firepower but the one with more stamina, more craft, skill and guile, more astute captaincy. The Middlesex captain, Adam Voges, put the gully fielder back to third man – would Middlesex regret this? The captain had the delicate dilemma between taking wickets and not leaking runs. Finn came to his aid at 1:39 when Clark was out caught behind on 31. A "bloodthirsty" crowd was rooting for Finn. Time therefore to dispense with third man? No. Lancashire now needed only 65 runs but were running out of batsmen, losing another at 1:53 (Bailey LBW Harris for three).

Unable to get the live camera coverage at The Oval back, I had to content myself with Twitter feeds: Surrey showing clips of the wickets falling in their innings; Somerset getting carried away with "SHOT! Bartlett crunches Dernbach through cover off back foot and ball races away for four" – but a picture would have been welcome; Lancashire, Yorkshire and Hampshire were reporting the wickets falling but no clips. Still, I could have no complaints about not being kept informed.

Lord's continued to supply the highest drama. At 1:59 Finn took his sixth wicket when Voges took a blinding catch to dismiss Jarvis for

nought. The ratcheting tension in the commentary box now turned to speculation as to whether Hameed would bat again.

At The Oval, at 2:24 Somerset had reached 51 for the loss only of Tresco. At Lord's Lancashire were still 54 runs off victory: was this a long way off or not? Yes, if you were a Lancashire supporter; no if you supported Middlesex. A Middlesex supporter of 75 years standing tweeted: "This match as stressful as travelling on Southern Rail."

At 2:27 Dawid Malan was back into the attack for Middlesex

with his leg-breaks, and McLaren, the No. 7, and Parkinson, the No. 11, were digging in. The burden of reaching victory was on McLaren's shoulders and by patient batting he was keeping Lancashire in the game. That is, as long as Finn was being rested, since at 2:46 he was back into the attack and eight minutes later had McLaren caught by the tall Rayner throwing his body backwards and hands skyward to take another extraordinary slip catch (see previous page). There was no better indication of Middlesex's will to win than the way Finn was bowling and the way catches were being held in the slips.

Lancashire now needed 38 runs with only their number 11 at the crease alongside their opener Hameed, severely disadvantaged by the injury to his hand. On the Somerset Twitter feed came the comment: "Come on Haseeb, make yourself a hero!" Someone else in Somerset tweeted that he was listening in his tractor, literally ploughing on and trying to avoid the telegraph poles. What Somerset needed was rain at Lord's, but at 3:04 it was all over when Parkinson was caught by Voges for 13, a notable score in the circumstances. This gave Finn final figures of 22.4-4-79-8, in a clear prod to the England selectors to consider him for the Ashes tour.

After this, the other games – for the first time – felt drained of colour. By the end of Day Three Somerset had got to 113-4. Byrom (39) and Bartlett (28) got in and got out. In Byrom's dismissal, Batty's off-break seemed just to have missed off stump, and while Batty indulged in a theatrical groan, Ben Foakes behind the wicket pointed out that the ball had clipped the off bail. I was struck by the way this scene rhymed with the way Porter got Dawson out on Day One (see page 20). Batting at No. 4, Hildreth (11) once again failed to make actual his potential ability. Abell (11*) and Davies (15*) had to do some serious batting on Day Four if Somerset were to salvage a draw. The weather had become gloomy at The Oval. Could it become gloomy on the next day and save Somerset?

At Leeds Warwickshire were 219 and 251, and Yorkshire 296 and 56-3, needing only 119 to win, advantage back to Yorkshire. At the Ageas Bowl, the game was swinging the champions away, since Essex (76 and 247-5) led Hampshire (254) by 69 runs.

DAY FOUR   Friday 21 September

The points table now looked like this:

Middlesex   143
Surrey   143
Hampshire   140
Yorkshire   129
Somerset   127.

On the face of it, Middlesex were safe, Surrey, grinding out victory, were about to be safe, Yorkshire were about to improve their position considerably. At the end of Day Four surely, the relegation battle would be between Hampshire and Somerset, with Somerset looking likely to go down. Tim Wigmore on Cricinfo reminded us that Somerset "have enjoyed ten unbroken years in Division One, the highest of any county". Did this mean that according to the Wheel of Fortune, it was their turn to go down? Or that it would be a shame to bring this record to an end?

In front of my PC on Friday, I thought the most interesting position in the four games was Essex's against Hampshire. Essex led Hampshire by 69 runs with five wickets in hand. In a way this looked straightforward: to win Hampshire had only to knock over the remaining five wickets and approach the run chase in a cool manner. But Essex were not champions for nothing. Collapsing for 76 all out in their first innings was a highly uncharacteristic moment. Following on in their second innings, Essex's 247-5 at the end of Day Three on the other hand was a platform to get to a sufficient score to unleash their bowling attack on the Hampshire second innings.

Tuning in to Radio Leeds before play started, I stumbled on a conversation taking place on air, although it was clear by the way the voices sounded remote and the commentators were setting out their stall that the microphone should have been off. A fruity Yorkshire voice was pronouncing that if Yorkshire were to lose, they would be right in the mire. I was struck by the fact that, since the commentator thought he was off air, he could have chosen much stronger language. This was admirable, what you hear is what you get. He then added, "They might do it if Ballance gets going." The weather should help also: by 10:45 the sun was casting shadows. The other Yorkshire news was that Ryan Sidebottom, the sidelined hero, was at Headingley to mark his final retirement from the team at their last home game. This should help to give the Yorkshire supporters a lift. In fact it worked all round: Sidebottom appeared after the match and was justly applauded for his achievements for Yorkshire. His place in the team had been taken by Patterson who, it turned out, made a crucial contribution. This was clearly the important game since it was the one chosen for broadcasting on Radio Five Live Sports Extra.

At 10:37 Fidel Edwards of Hampshire had the Essex captain, Ryan ten Doeschate, LBW for nine – the sixth wicket with Essex still only 74 runs ahead.

At 10:40 I found a live stream for The Oval. Decent shadows suggested poor weather was not about to come to Somerset's rescue. At 10:50 Abell was playing good cricket by leaving the ball outside off stump. Somerset's hopes rightly lay in attrition, in playing the game out, a superficially tedious process that masked countless inner tensions.

Things were soon happening, battles being won and lost. At Leeds, Ballance had not got going but was LBW to Jeetan Patel for 21, leaving Yorkshire 104 runs to win with six wickets in hand. Was this to be Patel's day? Then Essex were suddenly seven wickets down with only an 82-run lead. At 10:58 at The Oval Abell, playing less than good cricket, tentatively prodded at Clarke and was caught in the slips. Somerset were now on 132-5. The new bat was Peter Trego. Could he do something after five wickets in the Surrey innings yet an indifferent season overall? Was this his moment for redemption?

The commentators were beginning to speculate about the points table at the end of the day, and in Yorkshire speculation was turning to anxiety, since if they lost to Warwickshire they would only have 129 points, and if Somerset drew with Surrey they would have 132 points. Yorkshire would indeed be in the mire since for the final battle they were to confront champions Essex in Chelmsford, while Somerset would be inveigling Middlesex into the spider's lair at Taunton.

Tension was maintained by the run rates going down both at The

Oval and Headingley, where Patel bowled five maidens in a row. It was wisely said on the radio that you would not want to go back to the dressing room to explain how you got out to a rash shot. The risk was that in a negative mindset, you seemed to be waiting for the good ball to get you out. Overconfidence might in the end be just as defensible as underconfidence.

At 11:25 at Headingley Leaning was out to an excellent catch by Ian Bell off Patel and in front of their passionate, critical home crowd Yorkshire were 86-5. At 11:26 Essex's eighth wicket fell with only a 104-run lead. Might Yorkshire lose and Hampshire take themselves out of the relegation equation by winning? The wider public to these events was stirring. At 11:30 the radio told us there was a schoolgirl in Whitby listening in. I fondly envisaged her getting an unofficial but equally valuable education to the official one. Worse was to come for Yorkshire supporters: at 11:33 Tim Bresnan, just the player for these sort of circumstances, came down the track to Patel and was caught at midwicket. This was terrific spin bowling that was strangling the batsmen so that in their contortions to escape they succumbed. Patel was "unravelling the Yorkshire batting". And then at 11:44 Andy Hodd's wicket fell to the wrong Sidebottom to "a virtually soundless Headingley". They still needed 79 runs with three wickets remaining.

If they could have turned their minds elsewhere, they might have seen a glimmer of hope at the Ageas Bowl where Essex, although with only two wickets in hand were now 128 runs ahead. It was tweeted that with Fozzy (James Foster not out on 19) and Wags (Neil Wagner on 21 not out), Essex could start to get excited.

By high noon, Yorkshire needed only 61 with a minimum of 73 overs remaining, and a current run rate of 2.52. It all looked glacial provided you were not paying attention. It was not a matter of runs per over as in blast cricket, but of steel and grit to grind out the runs – or to grind out the wickets. Could Warwickshire continue to pressurize Yorkshire? Patel was slightly losing his line, while in Southampton Foster and Wagner were taking the game away from Hampshire.

At 12:18 Warwickshire missed a simple catch to short leg when the fielder, in turning away, might have caught it. Patterson (33, 131st game the Yorkshire) and Fisher (19, only fourth game for Yorkshire) were at the wicket: did they know the prognosis that rain was on its way? The 50th over was a tricky one from Patel (14-9-14-3 that morning) and Patterson tried a sweep shot three times without success. When lunch came at 12:32, Yorkshire were 141-7 needing 34 runs with Patterson not out 25 and Fisher not out 10 in a 45-run partnership. What was not going quite right for Warwickshire? According to the radio, the pace bowlers being a bit wide of off stump was a factor. More striking was the fact that they had given away 29 extras, having given away 32 in the first innings. The ball seemed to be scuttling through erratically, but surely this should be helping Warwickshire to take wickets as much as allowing Yorkshire to score extras?

Renewed hope for Yorkshire was bolstered by Essex's efforts. They were 362 all out at lunch, 184 runs ahead. It would take some fine Hampshire batting in the fourth innings to get these, but was it unlikely? That would be a rash conclusion.

These excitements had been dragging me away from The Oval, where the fight was far from over. That morning, having finally caught up with Surrey's total in their first innings at 11:40, the Somerset fringe of Davies and Trego had put on a good partnership of 66 runs when Davies fell at 12:10 to Batty for 52 runs. Could they possibly compile a score on a flat track to give their bowlers something to go at? In the 62nd over Trego was dropped off Dernbach and at 12:25 Overton struck a six off Batty. Going into lunch they were 220-6 with Trego and Overton engaged in battle on Somerset's behalf. Perhaps it was Surrey who welcomed the lunch break more to give them a rest and the opportunity to work out their tactics for the afternoon.

For my part, lunch was an expeditious sandwich before re-engaging with the cricket. At the Ageas Bowl 67 overs remained, enough for either Hampshire or Essex to get their way. At Headingley the Yorkshire fifty partnership between Patterson and Fisher came up with another no ball, and Patterson was definitely getting it right: 28 of his 34 had come from boundaries. At 1:27 Hampshire were suddenly 5-1, and possibly about to sink into the mire out of which Yorkshire was climbing. What is more, Patel was getting "a bit weary, understandably", as the radio put it. Two loose deliveries from him produced two lots of four leg-byes and at 1:46 Yorkshire only needed one run to win. Eight balls then passed with the scores level when Fisher, not yet battle-hardened and understandably perhaps a bit nervous, was caught at leg slip off Patel. There were only two wickets left for York-shire but Patterson, perhaps motivated in his testimonial year, was still there. The scores remained level for another 11 balls but then Patterson, choosing to twist rather than stick, and wisely discerning the correct ball on which to do so, struck a boundary. This gave him a match-winning innings of 44 not out, and the result meant Yorkshire had jumped to third in the Division One table behind Essex and Lancashire. Their supporters might not be going to enjoy it but the visit to Chelms-ford was going to be less stressful than envisaged when play started.

In Southampton, while Yorkshire was poised for victory, the Essex bowlers had begun their rampage. On the Essex Twitter feed breaking news was that Sam Cook, 20 years of age and still at Lough-borough University where he was preparing for the final year of his history degree, was known as 'Little Chef' to distinguish him from 'Chef', a.k.a. Alistair Cook. Why was he being talked about? Because he had removed the two Hampshire openers for one run apiece, and had just taken his third wicket, leaving Hampshire in a spin on 12 runs for four wickets. In five overs he had taken three wickets for nine runs.

Now followed a period of what in films is called parallel cutting between different scenes of action. At The Oval, Overton's had been the seventh wicket to fall on 234, and Trego, principal bearer of Somerset hopes, had been bowled at 242 for 68 precious runs but this Somerset innings needed a century-maker. Still, Bess and Leach were now at the crease and beginning to spin their batting muscles, putting together 23 runs from 62 balls. At 264-8, Somerset were one hundred runs ahead.

At the Ageas Bowl, poor footwork and shot selection by Hamp-shire was failing to repel Essex's precision bowling attack: they were 25-5 at 2:14, and five minutes later 29-6, when James Vince was LBW to Cook. It was only the fourteenth over of the innings.

At The Oval, Bess drove Dernbach for four in the 88th over, prompting the question why Clarke wasn't bowling, but as if in riposte to Batty's critics, at 2:27 Leach was caught by the aforementioned Clarke off the bowling of the Surrey captain, 39 years old and a wily campaigner who I imagine knew what he was doing. However perhaps telepathically he got the message because Clarke was brought into the attack. At 2:44 Somerset went from 299 to 303 with four leg-byes but at 2:49 Bess was caught by Foakes off Clarke for a fighting 35, and Somerset were 306 all out, leaving Surrey 143 to win. A minimum of 41.4 overs remained, so a minimum run rate of around 3.4 an over would be required. On a flat track Somerset were going to have to match Essex in throttling the batting but they lacked the equivalent firepower.

At the Ageas Bowl, that firepower was being relentless: Porter's second wicket had been Ervine (25-5); Vince had gone with the score on 29; Liam Dawson, the Hampshire spinner, had been bowled by Essex's more magic spinner, Simon Harmer, with his first ball. 37-7. Next to go was Berg and the score was 50-8. They were close to doom in this match, and the pundits were predicting a last-round shoot-out between Hampshire and Somerset. Hampshire then lost their ninth wicket with the score on 56 and at 3:32 their innings had folded with five wickets for Essex's Sam Cook, giving them victory by 108 runs. This was one of those matches that produced a pleasing symmetry: Hampshire 254, Essex 76, Essex 362, Hampshire 76.

On the Tuesday I had begun with four games to follow. At 3:35 p.m. on Friday there was one game standing on which all interested eyes could concentrate. Tea had been taken, and the next passage of play would be crucial. At 3:35 Somerset made a breakthrough when Burns was out caught in the deep with 38 runs on the board (below),

and then Stoneman with 39. But the force was with Surrey: considerable applause greeted Sangakkara walking to the wicket for his last home game. The crowd was building up and Surrey needed only 96 to win. "The major work is done, just admin to do now," as the radio commented. This was too facile, but somehow the idea that the game was on a knife-edge felt remote. Two left-hand batsmen brought Bess into the attack and he bowled a good first over, but then Somerset suffered a setback. Trego, their best bowler in the first innings, who had scored 68 with the bat in their second, was injured bowling his first ball and had to hobble off. Yet they were not without resources: Overton and Groenewald could be fiery, and Bess and Leach, who came on in place of Trego, could be clever. Abell wisely decided not to bowl himself. Bess was certainly motivated to compete, bowling in dark glasses which gave him a sinister quality, perhaps a necessary quality at this particular stage. Tresco went to short leg for Ryan Patel, 19 years old, and Bess used the breeze to drift it into the left-hander by tossing it up. Tightness and aggression were forcing Patel to bat from the crease and with the score on 73, he was bowled by Bess for 17.

Sangakkara was still there naturally, ticking along, when he was joined by Foakes. The substitute on the field for Trego, Roelof van der Merwe, who were he allowed to bowl would make spin triplets for Somerset, then had a word with Bess. Straight after, Foakes was dropped by Overton in a difficult catch low to his left (below).

With Surrey needing 56 runs, and with 18 overs remaining, Foakes was in positive mood, and began looking for boundaries while Sangakkara kept rotating the strike, thus slipping out of any stranglehold that Somerset might apply. In the 25th over, with 16 to go and one hour on the clock, Foakes hit two boundaries. The scales were tipping Surrey's way. Dot balls were harder to come by, and when Bess beat Foakes with the arm-ball, on the next ball Foakes hit him for six, a blast shot to demoralize bowler and opposition. The target was subsiding: in the 27th over, at 117-3, Surrey needed 26 to win; at the 28th over, 21 to win; 29th over, 18 to win; 30th over 15 to win. But on the first ball of the 31st over, Sangakkara hit Bess straight back as if aiming at the umpire's head - the umpire thought so too - and Bess struck out a hand and grabbed it (below).

Admiration for this remarkable piece of reaction cricket was then swept aside as the Somerset players ran over to shake Sangakkara's hand. Excessive? Other Sangakkaras will come along, surely? But in its way this gesture was exemplary.

Still, the end was nigh. Foakes, supported by Pope, who hit Bess for six and then four, cruised Surrey home, being 42 not out at the end with 30 of them coming in boundaries. The game had been a real bit of long-form wrestling, but as it was wisely commented, besides Sangakkara it was Clarke's bowling in the first innings that made the difference since "you have to score 400 runs in your first innings at The Oval".

The table now stood as follows:

Essex   228
Surrey   159
Lancashire 156
Yorkshire   145
Middlesex   143
Hampshire 140
Somerset   127
Warwickshire 78.

INTERLUDE - WEEKEND

Saturday and Sunday 23 and 24 September

Is there such a thing as a cricketsphere? The idea sounds plausible enough: 'a place where followers of cricket can gather to read and talk about cricket.' Although it might be doubted whether the County Championship was likely to be the first topic of conversation, yet at the weekend there was an online buzz of fascinated comment on what had happened from Tuesday to Friday, and on what to look forward to in the following week.

First of all, commentators spared a thought for Warwickshire: they had run Yorkshire close and it showed the quality to be found in the squad and in Division One. However their captain Jonathan Trott was hard-headed about his team: "Good enough to get in a position to win, not good enough to do it." Then on the BBC, he delivered another pithy comment: "It's nice to have players with potential, but potential is a very dangerous word until it's fulfilled." It prompted a memory of the Roman historian Tacitus's verdict on the Emperor Galba who lasted only seven months in the position – *capax imperii nisi imperasset* which can be paraphrased as 'potentially a ruler, until he actually ruled'.

The most pressing question was who would join Warwickshire in the relegation slot. Somerset seemed the prime candidate as they had to beat last year's champions and furthermore, they had to score more bonus points than Middlesex if they were to survive. Hampshire could save themselves from the drop if they could beat Warwickshire rather than draw with them.

The Division Two promotion race was increasing the buzz as well. The Northamptonshire v Nottinghamshire game just gone had produced a compelling result in the form of defeat for Nottinghamshire, thus putting both teams in contention for promotion. The position was that Worcestershire needed six points against Durham to claim the Division Two title. Nottinghamshire, were to visit Sussex, but they were only 13 points ahead of their rivals and with the more difficult game while Northamptonshire was to visit bottom-of-the-table

Leicestershire. Could a ninth win in the season take them over the line?

The most prominent story, however, was not the minutiae of the cricket but the rediscovery of a cricketing hero. Although the Sri Lankan star Kumar Sangakkara was due to play one more game for Surrey, the match at his home ground of The Oval was being seen as a valediction, one made all the lovelier by the poetry with which he meditated on the virtues of cricket: "I always tell the young Sri Lankan players, 'This is just a game.' But when you play in this game a lot, who you are as a person, your own values, your principles, all of that shines through. There is really no hiding-place on the cricket field. This is a unique game where players and personalities actually come through very honestly and clearly in the way they play. And not just play the game but the way they associate with their own team mates, but also the players that you play with and against. This has been a cornerstone of the game, and I'm happy that the Somerset boys thought I was worthy of coming and shaking my hand. That was very special to me." He concluded by saying he hoped to see "where my life takes me". On behalf of Somerset, in homage from the young to the seasoned, Tom Abell reciprocated: "You've got to appreciate genius when you see it." Not that King Kumar was Saint Kumar. The Cricinfo profile reminded readers that Sangakkara combined "a suave exterior with cutting asides and sharp sledges from behind the stumps [during his time as a wicket-keeper]". This was a fine weekend reflection, that he could spice his wisdom about cricket with wit on the field.

Ed Smith expatiated intelligently on the subject of Sangakkara in *The Sunday Times* and a study of his statistics for Surrey in 2017 showed how breath-taking they were. In 14 innings he had scored 1,442 runs at an average of 110.92, including eight centuries, five of them being consecutive. His scores through the season for Surrey were: 71, 46 and 136, 105, 114 and 120, 200 and 84, 4 and 26 (Essex spoiling the party), 180 not out, 164, 157 and 35. Surrey in fact so far had produced the three top scorers in Division One: Sangakkara 1,442, Mark Stoneman 1,034 (which had earned him a place in the England Test team) and Rory Burns 978. Surrey also had good bowlers as I had witnessed at The Oval, so one might reasonably conclude that the team was *capax* in terms of winning the County Championship, and that there was a hint of potential unfulfilled.

They had suffered too many draws (ten in the season so far) as had Middlesex, who as a result had got themselves into a position of considerable risk. It must be said that the playing-field in their case was not level with other counties, in fact it was decidedly capricious. To an extent they had to accept the pitch they were given at Lord's, and the busy schedule there meant the outground at Uxbridge came into play. This had proved a handicap in their game earlier in the month against Hampshire. The resulting scores were Middlesex 204 and 14-1 and Hampshire 146, the game petering out in the draw that might have produced a result if the pitch had not been so affected by the weather. At the end of August too they had been affected by something that won the prize for the most bizarre cricketing incident of the season, perhaps the decade. During the last day's play against Surrey at The Oval on 31 August a crossbow bolt was fired from outside the ground onto the field. The umpires took the players off, denying Middlesex the chance to improve their over-rate in the remainder of the final session. At the end of the match two penalty points were deducted from their total. Middlesex had discussions with the ECB to ask them to remove the penalty in view of the "unique and non-cricket related circumstances surrounding the match's abandonment". Their request was denied and they were informed that was no scope for any further appeal. Some wit dubbed the incident 'arrowgate', which is more euphonious if less accurate than 'boltgate', and as events unfolded it began to take on a larger significance.

So it came about that victory at Taunton was an imperative for Middlesex and even if victory was beyond them, at least the securing of bonus points. "Give us back our missing two points," must have been on the lips of many supporters. "This is just a game," sage Sangakkara had said, annoyingly.

For their part Somerset was facing relegation for the first time in a decade, and the 16-point gap between them and Middlesex looked like an abyss. The countycricketsphere had had much to relish, with the prospect of more to come. Abell called the game a "cup final".

INTERLUDE - GALLERY

Slow cricket may seem largely to consist of nothing happening, yet less casual acquaintance reveals that it is a game of explosive action that compensates for all the preceding inaction and is made possible by the way that inaction in fact masks a gathering of energy: the bowler resting the body even as he plots the next ball, the batsman dialling down concentration before dialling it up again, the fielders relaxing before tensing again, the umpires mentally preparing their senses and their minds for the next ball. Only the captain can never relax but instead use this 'inaction' to check field placings, consider the next bowling moves, ensure that he has taken account of everything – the state of the pitch, the condition of the ball, even the mindset of the players including that of opponents.

Photography is a superlative medium for capturing cricketers at work. Degas, the nineteenth-century French painter, revolutionized the painting of motion, notably that of ballet dancers and race horses, by seeing it <u>photographically</u>, photography *avant la lettre*, so to speak – search Degas on Google Images for evidence. This vision has been taken up by sports photography and been supercharged so that it now flourishes around the world. Here is a gallery of images from Day Two (Surrey v Somerset) and Day Six (Essex v Yorkshire) freezing the bodily contortions that cricketers perform in between the moments of inaction.

Tim Groenewald

Craig Overton

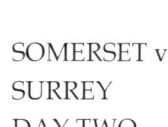

balletic Overton

SOMERSET v
SURREY
DAY TWO

Peter Trego

Trego's hand

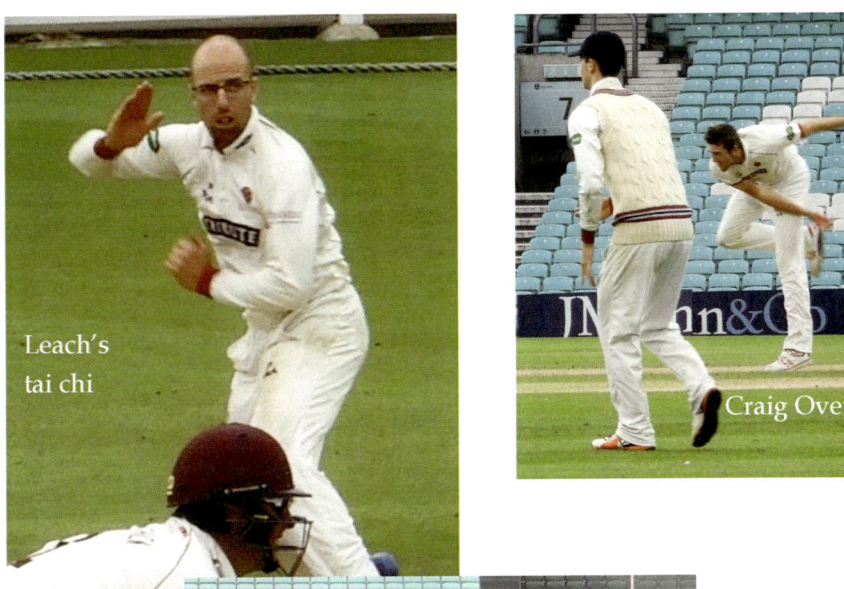

Leach's tai chi

Craig Overton's force

Dom Bess and Jack Leach skipping

Bess's hands in prayer

Bess's leap of faith

Ben Foakes from back. . .

. . . and front

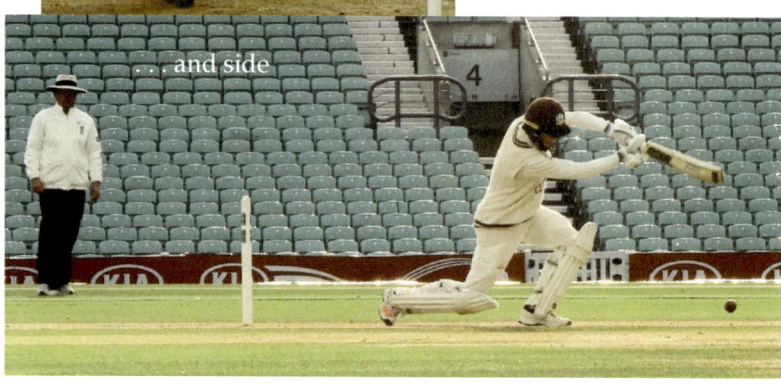

Ollie Pope from back . . .

. . . and side

ESSEX v YORKSHIRE DAY SIX

Jamie Porter flexed . . .

. . . and sideways

Neil Wagner goes horizontal

Wagner straining

Wagner leaping

← Simon Harmer tosses it up

Essex slips alert to Harmer

Matt Fisher crowded by and
defensive to Harmer

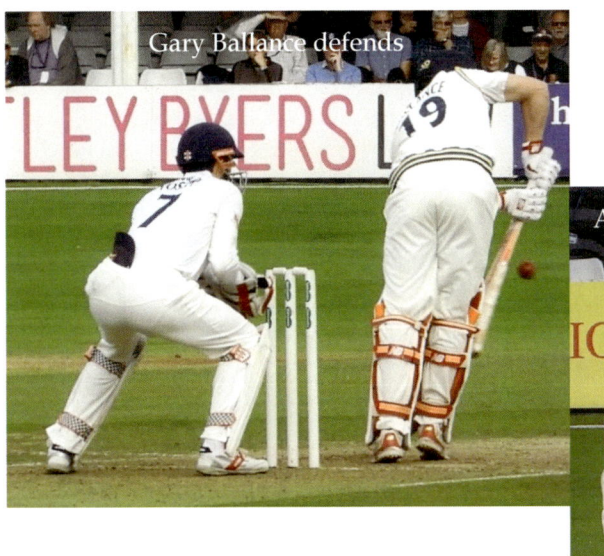

Gary Ballance defends

Adam Lyth poised

Adam Lyth at crease

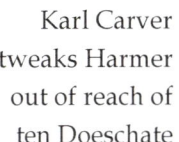

← Andy Hodd driving and missing

Karl Carver tweaks Harmer out of reach of ten Doeschate

Yorkshire slips getting excited

Nick Browne in control

Dan Lawrence a blur

Steve Patterson's arm a blur

Ben Coad's skating

Adam Lyth's twist

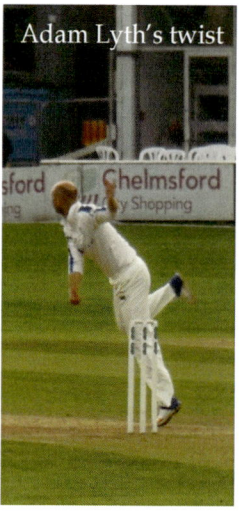

DAY FIVE   Monday 25 September

The BBC website laid out the stall for us: 1) Somerset had to beat Middlesex to stand a chance of staying up; 2) Middlesex needed nine points to guarantee safety, comprising three bowling points, five points for a draw and scoring at least 200 to secure one batting point; 3) Hampshire needed 12 points against Warwickshire; 4) Yorkshire needed seven points against Essex. History must record as well a fourth game of Lancashire v Surrey at Old Trafford, but its result had no bearing on the Championship, although the question arose of whether Sangakkara would depart from county cricket with a bang or a whimper.

You could throw 'arrowgate' into this mix. Supposing Middlesex had not had two points deducted, the task for Somerset would have been even more massive. If that had been the case, then technically, Somerset could leapfrog Middlesex by winning at Taunton, with three bowling points and maximum batting points, making a total of 151 points, while denying Middlesex any batting points and, if possible, bowling points. Winning the toss and scoring 400 in under 110 overs in the first innings (if possible without losing all their wickets), would tee Somerset up to then dismiss Middlesex for under 200 in their first innings, making them follow on and then dismissing them again. Middlesex, starting on 145 points, would only get three bowling points for a

The County Ground, Taunton, with St James's

total of 148. The scenario was a preposterous one, and it was all exerting pressure on my brain albeit in a pleasurable enough way.

So, there was only one game to follow, the one at Taunton. In any case, the Warwickshire v Hampshire match was delayed by rain, as was the Essex v Yorkshire game, although Essex were surely going to beat, perhaps trounce Yorkshire. So, the cup final it had to be.

In view of the pitch's green tinge, a tweet on the Middlesex stream commented, "Not sure we're looking at a four-day wicket." The toss was important, and Somerset promptly won it, an act of immense kindness from the cricketing gods, consigning the question 'What if Middlesex had won it?' to the dustbin. They were batting and the first over was bowled by Andrew Murtagh to Methuselah Trescothick, 41 years and 274 days old. Their team had no Peter Trego who was injured but it did have three spinners in Bess, Leach and Van der Merwe to backup Overton and Groenewald, a full house as it were, comprising three of a kind and a pair. Middlesex's bowling attack was three quicks (Murtagh, Finn, Harris) and three slows (Stirling, Malan, Ravi Patel), who were undoubtedly *capax* but could they fulfil their potential?

For Somerset, Tresco and Byrom were setting about their task, and at 12:22 Byrom made his first fifty in first-class cricket, including 11 fours, a good moment to do it. Then Stirling came on and in the 31st over, at 12:28, he had Byrom caught at slip for 56. On the radio Anthony Gibson, the Somerset specialist, commented that it was much the best he had seen Byrom bat so that was evidence of motivation. We were also told that Trescothick had signed on for yet another season, remaining hungry to win the County Championship before joining Sangakkara in the cricketing Elysian Fields.

It was only at 12:30 that I found a live stream of the game on the Middlesex Twitter feed at CricHQ.tv, at which point they went off for lunch with Somerset on 93-1. Elsewhere, rain continued to delay Warwickshire v Hampshire and at Chelmsford, where play had started, Essex had stuttered from 63-2 to 84-5 which was the score at a 1 PM lunch, Yorkshire doing themselves proud. But the relentless focus was on Taunton where the lunch interval allowed everyone to gaze at the pitch (see next page). After lunch Patel and Malan were on, although Malan only got three overs in the Somerset innings. Patel, in his second

game of the summer, was the threat and bowled a quick, flat ball at Tresco well outside off stump and had him LBW for 37. The image below shows Patel 'looking round the corner' to check that the job is done.

This allowed another tandem of innocence and experience in the form of 19-year old George Bartlett and the 33-year old James Hildreth. Hildreth had had a haircut over the weekend. Was he seeking a different, more successful persona for this crucial game? They needed to carry on accumulating, and at 1:52 Bartlett hit a six off Patel, only to be bowled round his legs at 2:07 for 25. Somerset were 139-3. This brought to the crease Tom Abell, forced by circumstances to combine relative innocence and experience since he was a 23-year-old captain. Amid this tension, the fact that Sangakkara was out for 14 at Old Trafford seemed only a footnote.

For me that tension was being dislocated – or possibly enhanced – by the fact that the commentary on the Radio Five Live web broadcast was two balls behind the live stream, so I was seeing the action before hearing it described. But if I listened to my DAB radio with the screen commentary mute, I was hearing the action before seeing it. I agonised over which was better, and felt that while neither was perfect, it was more satisfactory to see and then hear than to hear and then see, to know with the eye before imagining with the ear rather than imagining it and then knowing it. Those thoughts particularly applied to the run out of Abell by Patel. Abell, quick between the wickets, turned for a second run only for Hildreth to send him back, and only for Abell to slip and thus be caught out of his crease.

Middlesex had crucially dented Somerset's momentum at 176-4. At 3:11 Adam Voges, the Middlesex captain, gave himself an over, and when the sides went in for tea, Somerset were 193-4 after 67 overs, at a run rate of 2.88. One batting point looked certain and two eminently achievable. More than 300 would give them three. Middlesex may have run out Abell but, the radio told us, they had dropped four catches two of them "pretty straightforward".

Resuming after tea, Somerset reached 200 at 3:39. At 3:45 there were only nine overs to the new ball. Whether to take this was hard to evaluate because all the wickets so far had fallen to spin, principally that of Patel. Voges would not necessarily want to change this, a point confirmed when in the 73rd over Hildreth was LBW to Patel for 41, and next ball Van der Merwe was caught in the slips. On the live chat stream, football partisanship was breaking out: "Van der Merwe never touched it. . ." "It's rigged . . ." ". . . missed it by miles". Really these were squeals of pain in protest at the fact that Somerset were now 206-6, and Middlesex were eyeing a Somerset collapse. Apart from Byrom (56) and Hildreth (41) none of the Somerset batsmen had reached 40.

In truth the spinners were extracting bounce and turn, and

Patel's figures of 64-4 meant he was enjoying the Taunton pitch more than anyone else on the Middlesex side. At 3:59 Overton, forced to stick, was caught in the slips for one, and at 4:02 Stirling had his second wicket when Bess, choosing to twist, holed out to Finn for nought. Somerset were now 214-8. This little passage of play created its own drama, since Middlesex were desperate to prevent Somerset getting a second batting point: if Somerset got 250, Middlesex would have to score 300 in reply.

I felt that in Somerset heads the psychological battle to get to 250 was preventing them from doing so. At one end Steve Davies was holding up patiently, and his new partner, Jack Leach, perhaps knew no other way than to bat patiently, until, that is, at 4:25 he holed out to Finn off Patel, the ninth wicket down and Somerset still 20 runs from that second point. Davies had to take it to the bowlers but six runs later he died to a slip catch off Patel for 27, giving the bowler first-innings figures of 29.4-3-81-7. Somerset were 236 all out, and the radio verdict was that this was disastrous for Somerset, whose last six wickets had fallen for 31 runs, and great for Middlesex. If they could get to 250 and garner two batting points they would end up above Somerset <u>even if they lost</u>.

Elsewhere, play at Edgbaston had been abandoned for the day, while, just as Somerset had travailed at Taunton, Essex were 183-8 in the 59th over. The game against Yorkshire looked like being a real contest, and this was encouraging because I had decided to go to Chelmsford on the second day of the game in order to see mighty Essex for myself, and be back at my PC for Days Three and Four of the Taunton game. I had in fact agonized whether to make the effort to get to Taunton for Day Two, and possibly Day Three, but the travelling and the cost were a deterrent. Anyway, Chelmsford is a good deal easier to reach from Norwich and since I was able to watch the Taunton game online, why not stay fully involved that way?

Just as Middlesex were to start their innings, and as if to re-motivate the two teams, not that that showed any signs of wilting, it was announced on Twitter around 4:44 that Yorkshire, as a result of their three points from bowling Essex out, while Somerset had only got one batting point, had achieved the swing they needed and thus

Division One cricket in 2018 was secured. The fight to avoid relegation was now down to three teams.

At 4:40 the Middlesex innings got under way with the dependable Overton, who had been at it all season, bowling at Sam Robson. Conventional enough, but then at the River End, the new ball was given to Leach to spin the first over at Nick Compton. On the sixth ball of the over, it turned, bounced, spat – and triggered a big appeal. Compton however fell to pace not spin: at the end of the third over, he was out to a catch behind off Overton. Compton had taken a while to take guard, as if he intended to wind up the bowler, something he did so successfully that Overton fired the ball in at his fastest, Compton had still not woken up sufficiently, and the batsman had suffered as a result.

This was the first wicket to fall to seam in the day, but it was only the joker in the pack. Spin was trumps, and Leach, pitching on off stump was making "every ball feel like a wicket", according to the radio. There was a certain inevitability in Eskinazi in the sixth over and Robson in the eighth succumbing to 'caught Trescothick'.

MID TRAIL 232 | 4/1 | OVER 5.0 | Leach to Eskinazi

MID TRAIL 231 | 5/2 | OVER 7.3 | Leach to Robson

Getting plenty of bounce, Leach was made by Middlesex to look almost unplayable. At 5:12, Leach's figures were 5-4-2-2, with four overs left in the day.

The new bat was Dawid Malan, who was to prove his resilience and skill in the Ashes series in the winter, and Abell brought on Bess, bowling leg-breaks to the left-hand bat. However, Bess did not achieve as much control as Leach, and Malan using his feet began to dig in.

It was almost the end of the day, but there was one bizarre vignette yet to come – although perhaps to Somerset supporters it had lost its novelty because they had seen it before. Van der Merwe was brought on, and the live stream showed Tresco fielding at second slip on his knees. Although nothing could be more reasonable, as he is a big man and over all those seasons his knees must have been made to work hard and were therefore crying out for relief, the sight was enough to elicit a gasp.

At Taunton, play ended after 15 overs of the Middlesex innings, with Malan on nine and Voges four not out. 13 wickets had fallen on Day One, and the post-tea session produced nine wickets for 48 runs. By 6:14 Voges had made his opinions known to the Cricket Liaison Officer regarding the pitch, and we were informed that this official would be having a discussion with the umpires and giving more information on Day Two. This was highly important for Somerset as a points deduction would see them being relegated even if they won the game.

For my part I like watching spin bowling, and feel we do not get enough of it. On Cricinfo, George Dobell gave a measured weighing up of the contentions at stake, but produced the decisive point in favour of the pitch: "[the pitch] continued to reward merit rather than chance and was probably no harder than the conditions England faced in Dhaka at the end of [2016] and similar to those experienced towards the end of games. in India. If county cricket exists, in part at least to prepare players for such challenges, perhaps such surfaces should be encouraged?" The fact that England were to lose the Ashes over the winter later produced heart-searching about the difficulty they had in winning away from home. Finding good spinners in county cricket, and learning how to play them, seems even more urgent than ever.

Tempers, so inimical to sport, were perhaps rising at Taunton and so a blissed-out day at Chelmsford beckoned all the more. Bad light had put an end to play with Essex 227 all out. Could Yorkshire exceed this total sufficiently to exert pressure on the champions, and uplift their supporters at the end of the season? Their argument would be that a side that has won the championship could be demotivated.

DAY SIX   Tuesday 26 September

I thought I had arrived at Chelmsford station in time to see the first ball of the day, but the entrance to the ground is via a crooked path through a bijou park, under a dark road bridge spanning the river Can, and then to a sombre kiosk pointing Members one way, the public another. It was certainly not an infernal case of 'Abandon hope all you who enter here', but more exactly, 'Abandon all hope of getting into the ground quickly.' Still, I was inside on the second over to find Porter and Cook bowling to Lyth and Brathwaite, and to feel an expectation like a scent in the air. Spectators were turning up, and while you could never call it a raucous crowd, it was gazing at play raptly. Essex's success seemed to have drawn supporters out to watch them in action. I heard one exchange take place behind me. The first voice said, "It was good Essex winning the County Championship." Second voice: "They try hard, bless 'em."

At 11:07 the stumps went flying when Brathwaite hit the ball dead straight down the ground only for it to be fielded by the stumps. But Yorkshire were finding batting no easier than Essex had the day before. Essex had a fine quartet of bowlers on: Jamie Porter, Sam Cook, Simon Harmer, Neil Wagner. The last two were their overseas players, and Harmer had been crucial to their success, but the first two were

home-grown, from Leytonstone and Chelmsford. In fact ten of the players in their squad were home-grown, five from Leytonstone.

At 11:50 Porter bowled Brathwaite (see previous page), and very soon after, Harmer was on. His first ball Lyth hit for four, and his second for six, seeking to blunt Harmer's lethal intent. But only four minutes later, Harmer had Lees caught at the wicket for four off 11 balls. Harmer's intent (below) did not seem blunted.

In fact, the Yorkshire batsmen came and went and although there was some resistance, wickets fell at regular intervals: 11:15 AM (11th over), 11:32 (14th), 11:43 (17th), 11:51 (19th), 12:09 PM (23rd), 12:35 (31st), then lunch, 1:55 (41st), 2:02 (42nd), 2:06 (43rd) and 2:18 (46th). Yorkshire strived to resist: Brathwaite concentrated hard for his four off 28 balls; Lyth made 35 off 53 balls, Hodd 21 off 33 balls; just after lunch Fisher and Patterson tried repeating their heroics of the previous week by holding Essex back, Fisher making nine off 63 balls and Patterson five off 26, but to no avail.

The Essex force was against them, and so was hazard: Ballance, seeking to continue to prove his worth to the England selectors, had scored 13 runs off 26 balls when Hodd hit Wagner hard down the pitch, only for Wags to bend down sharply, get his fingers on the ball deftly

playing Harmer

Ballance gropes

Hodd reverse-sweeps

Fisher square-drives

and divert it onto the stumps skilfully, with the ball still travelling hard enough to send the stumps flying (see sequence of images on previous page). Fortune or skill? Wagner was jubilant, understandably, and to my eye could take some credit for the swiftness of his reaction. "Cricketers make their own luck." Whatever, it gave us a glimpse of the spectacular, and there is something thrilling about stumps and bails flying.

In the early afternoon a sergeant-major voice, surely familiar to Yorkshire devotees, called out, "C'mon Yorkshire!" to which an Essex woman was ready: "Yes, c'mon Yorkshire, give us a game!"

At 2:10 Ben Coad hit a four to bring up 100 runs, and then I caught ten Doeschate and Harmer conferring.

Harmer's next ball had Carver caught at the wicket and Yorkshire were 111 all out, with three wickets each for Porter, Harmer and Wagner.

That was the first half of a champion performance. Could they now capitalise on being 116 runs ahead on the first innings? At first it looked not, when Chopra was LBW to Brooks for four in the third over. The image shows the slips appealing successfully. Two balls later Bopara was out LBW for nought. That brought Dan Lawrence to the

crease to join Nick Browne and these two began industriously to repair the innings. Industry included patience: only 21 runs were scored off 11 overs, a run rate of 1.9 an over which then dropped to 1.6 an over. Lawrence took 54 balls to hit his first boundary. Browne had been aided by Brathwaite dropping a sharp chance off him in the slips, but the pressure still seemed to be more on the batsmen than the bowlers.

After tea, I had hoped to get into the Members' stand but the game was too well attended for that to be allowed, and I had to be content with a view behind mid-off looking into a September evening sun and cloud, a field of glory effect. In the image below the glint on Lawrence's bat makes it look like a sword blade.

Resistance by Browne and Lawrence was beginning to pay off and the run rate was creeping back up to two runs an over.

At 4:58 Browne took Essex to 100 with a four, and in the evening

shadows batting seemed more benign. At 5:09 Lawrence (above) reached his fifty, and at 5:30 Browne did the same. Soon after, the players came off for bad light with the score on 134-2 off 48 overs, at an overall run rate of 2.8. Essex were now 250 runs ahead, eight wickets in hand, and firmly in charge.

Having spent the day juggling my cameras, binoculars, notebook, coffee and snacks, I had purposely avoided any hot line as to what was happening in the other games. When I got home I felt the

thrill of anticipation in finding out.

There had been sun at Edgbaston, so play started there with Hampshire needing eight points to survive in Division One. It seemed straightforward enough when they had Warwickshire 28-5, but Sibley then resisted, scoring 92 not out in Warwickshire's total of 188. Because so much was at stake for Hampshire, his achievement was soured in their eyes when he sought to hit Mason Crane for six. Unfortunately George Bailey was awaiting on the boundary. John Culley on Cricinfo described the moment thus: "Bailey [sensed] his momentum would carry him over the boundary after a running leap for the ball at long-off and [opted] to flick it back into the air one-handed. He then caught it cleanly with both hands but then there was the matter of where his landing foot was at the moment of first contact." The umpires, reasonably enough, had not seen it precisely, nor was a television replay available. Bailey felt he knew, i.e. it was a legitimate catch; Sibley demurred and claimed a six. In the end he was given the benefit of the doubt. This was one of cricket's ticklish moments. You could sense Bailey's first thought that he had caught it, and perhaps his second: "C'mon Warwickshire, you're relegated, we are in a big fight." On the other hand, it did also feel academic since shortly after this incident the Warwickshire innings ended at 188 all out. Sibley was 92 not out instead of caught Bailey bowled Crane 84. Not a big deal – except it was, for honour, personal success and the spirit of cricket were all in play. I could see everyone's point of view.

Matters were in Hampshire's hands, and they promptly made life much harder for themselves when they were dismissed for 116, no batsman scoring more than 16 except for Bailey with 55. Although a whole day had been lost to poor weather, Hampshire had no batting points and a whole two days to eke out a draw, their requirement being five points now they had secured the three bowling ones. Alternatively they could lose but be rescued by Somerset failing to beat Middlesex. As one knew all along, it was the conclusion of events at Taunton that were top of the agenda.

The Taunton facts on Day Two are baldly stated: at the end of it, Middlesex had gone from 18-3 to 142 all out, and Somerset at the close of play were 159-3. The advantage was emphatically Somerset's: Somerset had denied Middlesex a batting point, or the pitch had denied them, depending on your point of view; they were 253 runs ahead; it looked as if the weather was going to allow the match to go the full distance; and as a Somerset supporter might have sung in their bath, "Whatever happens we have got / the spinning guns and they have not." Would this be fair on the Middlesex spinners? Not in Patel's case whose figures were 81-7 in the first innings, plus a run out, and who was up for doing it all again in the second. Although Stirling had taken two wickets in the first innings, he was an all-rounder who had aided the Middlesex cause by top-scoring in their innings, and the situation needed a specialist spinner.

I turned to George Dobell on Cricinfo, who pointed out that Nathan Sowter, the Middlesex leg-spinner, had been named in the original squad but left out of the team. He then added drily: "Adam Voges might have found more assistance in the surface if he had landed the ball on it more often." However even Voges knew this by only bowling three overs in the Somerset second innings. Of Patel, Dobell commented that in delivering over the wicket and pitching down the leg side, "he often asked the ball to do too much." Finally, the brevity of Middlesex's innings at 50.3 overs had not allowed the bowlers time to recover, a point made by the Middlesex bowler James Harris. In long-form cricket arm-wrestling needs to be used to wear down an opponent, and Middlesex had failed to do so.

It is a beauty of the game, conventionally said but no less true for that, that it wonderfully combines individual performance with that of the team. This was a game in which the side that produced the big innings would triumph. In timely fashion, James Hildreth obliged. Tresco had chipped in with 31 runs off 65 balls, an opener's contribution that provided a platform on which Hildreth could build his innings, being 82 not out at the day's end. He was quoted as saying: "I don't think the pitch has eased. If the spinners put it in the right areas, it is still tough. Half the battle as a batter is in your head. If you come on to this sort of wicket and think it's really hard work, you've probably shot yourself in the foot. Guys who have applied themselves in both innings have shown there are runs to be had out there."

So Hildreth's innings, which was apparently chanceless,

showed it was possible to bat well on this supposedly controversial pitch. In truth, the furore over the pre-match preparation should not have been about the physical matter of the pitch, but the psychological one of the players' minds. Even though it was their home ground so they were used to it, Somerset seemed to be better prepared mentally. Abell had flourished by taking his time and providing key support for Hildreth, prompting the quote of the day from Dobell: "It is the shots you don't play that are as valuable as those you do."

Middlesex were fired up, undoubtedly, but Somerset clearly more so. In the 18th over of Middlesex's 51-over innings, Simpson was run out by Bess throwing down the stumps from the covers, i.e. aiming at a single stump. All cricketers practise this a lot but for every practice hit there is surely a practice miss. But Bess's practising made him luckier, it seems, aided perhaps by those dark glasses he wears, which had been derided by a Surrey spectator at The Oval with, "Don't forget the sunglasses when the sun comes out." In a way the last laugh was with Bess.

DAY SEVEN   Wednesday 27 September

So - Somerset stay up if they beat Middlesex; a Middlesex win or draw keeps them and Hampshire safe; Hampshire are relegated if they lose and Somerset win.

Motivation was to the fore. Another minor one occurred this day when Somerset's Craig Overton got called up to the England squad, and Middlesex's Steven Finn did not. This decision had nothing to do with events at Taunton, but it cannot but have buoyed spirits in the Somerset dressing room.

As play started, the live chat on the Somerset streaming of the game was that Somerset might look to declare before lunch giving them some time to bowl at Middlesex before the rain predicted for the afternoon actually arrived. Finn's rhythm was initially absent, since in his first over there were three fours from Hildreth, including a cut hit with both feet off the ground, and at the end of the first two overs, Somerset had added 18 runs to their score. However Patel proved himself still committed to the Middlesex cause when he had his second wicket with Abell caught at slip. Abell's 45 off 123 balls looked modest at first glance but was a captain's innings, and the 126-run partnership with Hildreth marked the decisive swing of the match in Somerset's favour even if they were to lose wickets. Hildreth was still there in any case, reaching his hundred at 11:05. Four minutes later Patel had Davies LBW.

There had been some slow handclapping at the ground the reason for which at my distant station I could not discern, but perhaps marking a latent anxiety that rain would deny Somerset victory by gifting Middlesex a draw, so they wanted Middlesex to hurry up. This began to seem remote as there was a day and a half to go. But Roelof Van der Merwe caught the mood by hitting a six in the 72nd over. The next over, Hildreth was bowled by Harris for 109, but his departure only made Van der Merwe accelerate. His batting style being of the blast persuasion, he had 17 so far off 10 balls.

The Somerset live chat was beginning to get aggressive, unpalatable even, in the way social media can turn private obscenities into public ones. Look away from them, I had to tell myself. Fortunately events on the pitch remained compelling. Overton tried to slog Patel and was stumped.

SOM	226/6	OVER	Patel to C Overton	MID
LEAD 320		73.3		142

Bess came in and soon he and Van der Merwe were scampering between the wickets; but at 11:39 Bess was LBW Murtagh. Their partnership was only 11 but its passage of eight balls conveyed the urgency: Overton out (73.4 overs), three, one, nought, one, two, three, one, Bess out. Bess's innings had taken eight minutes but in a way time seemed to stand still. Then at 11:42 Van der Merwe was out attempting a reverse slog, caught Finn bowled Patel for 24 in 19 balls, including two fours and one six. Patel was certainly kindled by the batsmen taking a charge at him: he now had five wickets.

When Bess fell, Somerset were 331 runs ahead, which was surely enough. Abell might boldly have declared but sensibly enough carried on: a lead of 350 would feel perfect. Anyway Leach fancied things: at 11:51 he hit Patel over long on for six, the ball disappearing through the door of the first tier of the Botham stand. A moment later, Somerset declared on 250-9, leaving Middlesex 344 to win, or bat out the match. Ravi Patel, keen as mustard, had 12 wickets in the two innings.

This break was an opportunity to catch up elsewhere. Essex were now leading Yorkshire by 336 runs with five wickets remaining, forging ahead in their pomp. At Edgbaston the game continued on its own knife edge. Warwickshire (188 and 65-4) led Hampshire (116) by 137 runs. They still had six wickets left and seemed motivated to bring off their first win of the season. Ian Bell I noted was on 18 not out so could he help do so?

Taunton: the match was restarting, and the players were banishing all risk of dullness. Overton's first ball Compton pushed into the off and then set off for a suicidal run. Overton collected and threw to the wicket-keeper's end, just missing running out Sam Robson. Nerves of steel were required, not nerves of jelly, especially as rain was definitely on the way. Weather information was prominent on the Somerset Twitter feed, but so far Taunton remained an island of dryness.

Edgbaston: Warwickshire were 70-5, 142 ahead, with five wickets left.

Taunton: Leach's spin came on in the second over, as it had on Day One, but Somerset themselves were not immune from nerves. In the fourth over, bowled by Leach, Robson's bat gave the "simplest of simple catches" according to the radio, but the ball still popped out of Abell's hands. At 12:20 Van der Merwe was on, and at 12:25 we had sight of Tresco on his knees in the slips (see below at left), although the radio told us that he was yet to take a catch in that position.

When the ball came sharply off the bat and went through him, he moved even nearer. Then in the eighth over, Leach struck by having Robson caught by Overton in the slips, with the guilty Abell the first to congratulate Leach. At lunch Middlesex were 21-1, 324 runs from their target of 345. The task must have felt massive to them and they especially needed a curmudgeonly innings from Compton to take them through to the close of play. Yet there was a sense that the turning, bouncing pitch had got into the minds of Middlesex's batsmen, as if Somerset had a twelfth man in play.

Edgbaston: Warwickshire were 95-6, a lead of 167 runs. It was commented that 200 should be a minimum target, setting Hampshire 273 runs to win. What is more Ian Bell was still there.

Taunton: shortly after play resumed, Compton's resistance came to an end when he was LBW to Leach for 10 off 46 balls. This brought the left-handed Malan to the crease so Bess immediately started limbering up to pitch his laser-guided off breaks at the footmarks. And then, late in the fortnight, I enhanced my pleasures of spectatorship by some judicious experimental pausing of the flow of play onscreen, finally matching up the visual live stream with the commentary. At 1:30 Bess's first ball was the arm ball, a nice piece of bluff, but the second ball was an orthodox off-break to the left-hander and Malan was gone caught Davies bowled Bess for nought.

The new bat was Adam Voges, who managed to survive with Eskinazi, now 16 not out, properly digging in until the rain finally reached Taunton at 1:43. I was dismayed that the game had to stop but the delicious part of it was that by switching attention to Edgbaston I could still watch cricket, and I could renew interest as well in what was happening at Chelmsford.

So I found a Warwickshire live stream courtesy of CricHQ.tv, although I could not move the image to full-screen, and I had difficulty in pausing it to enjoy those frozen moments that cricket is so good at providing, when the crucial moment, although it is in time, you can take out of time. Warwickshire were now 127-8, a competitive lead of 199, but then Edwards clean bowled Hannon-Dalby. Ian Bell, still at the crease, had to get a move on, which he promptly did. At 1:56 he hit a six, at 2:03 he reached his 50, at 2:06 he hit his second six. He had finally found his fluency, largely missing all season, with the ability that showed true class to take boundaries even though fielders were set back to encourage singles. 11 minutes after reaching his fifty, he was on 73. He was ably supported in this effort by Sidebottom, but his 13 off 32 balls came to an end at 2:46 with Warwickshire 186 all out and Bell 77 not out. Hampshire now needed 259 runs to win, perfectly feasible since there were over four sessions to do it in, but they must also have concluded that the pitch allowed scope for a draw. The danger man was the Warwickshire spinner Jeetan Patel. Like his Taunton counterpart and namesake, could he unleash any gremlins in the pitch and any gremlins in the minds of the Hampshire batsman? Hampshire were perhaps aided in an obscure way by the thought that Somerset might win at Taunton, which would be a lesser threat to their status than a Middlesex win.

At Chelmsford Essex had declared on 334-7 after several of their batsmen had made hay of the Yorkshire bowling: Browne 83, Lawrence 83, ten Doeschate 57, Harmer 58. This must have been a source of dismay to the Yorkshire supporters at the ground, with the prospect of this deepening when Essex unleashed their attack on the batsmen. So it proved: in the interval at Edgbaston, an Essex live stream showed Yorkshire 17-3. At 3:15, Yorkshire were 33-5, with Sam Cook taking four wickets for some 13 runs, wickets falling in the second, third, sixth, eighth and twelfth overs. Yorkshire may have been batting in the Elysian sunshine, but this was surely excruciating for Yorkshire fans considering that, bar Brathwaite who had been out for one run, all the batsmen had figured so prominently in their championship title victory of 2015: Lyth, Lees, Ballance, Leaning. Four minutes from tea, Hodd had been out reverse-sweeping Harmer and Yorkshire were 35-6. On the radio could be heard the laments of the commentator Dave Callaghan, scrupulously polite, deeply informed, of long experience at a microphone, and most strikingly, unostentatiously but openly partisan for Yorkshire. "Where's the pride?" he lamented. I could not help but feel for them, even if the other half of the picture was the quality of Essex's cricket. In the first ball after tea, Porter had Patterson caught at the wicket for two. It was hard to see the next batsmen, the effervescent Jack Brooks, gritting it out and in the next over he gave Cook his fifth wicket. Porter, Harmer and Wagner had bowled well; Cook had bowled superlatively. It was left to the Yorkshire new boys to offer resistance. Matthew Fisher made 25 off 48 balls and Karl Carver nine off 33 balls. When Fisher was tenth man out in the 29th over, Yorkshire had sunk like a failed soufflé to 74 all out. The light was declining rapidly, but the ground had at least 3000 spectators, at least half the capacity, to watch Essex seal victory and remain unbeaten all season, a notable achievement.

When tea came at Edgbaston, Hampshire were 20-1, and then rain came to their aid. This was frustrating for Warwickshire who were losing time to bowl at Hampshire. When you are at the opposite end of the scale from Essex somehow ill-fortune dogs you: can you be said to make your own ill luck?

. At Taunton the rain continued, so the table for the relegation candidates now stood:

(Yorkshire   148)
Middlesex   146
Hampshire   143
Somerset   131.

A win for Somerset would take them to 147, a point above Middlesex, a draw for Hampshire to 148, two points above Middlesex. That crossbow incident at The Oval was likely to be causing pain in London. The news was now surfacing that, allegedly, the umpires in that game had been told that Middlesex would declare and then make up the over rate. Then the bolt from the blue occurred. . .

DAY EIGHT   Thursday 28 September

I had become so enthralled by what was happening in these county games that I felt cricket fans in the rest of the country should urgently be alerted to them. I had been quite disconcerted by the week's cricket headlines: an early-morning fracas in Bristol on Monday 25 September involving Ben Stokes was a journalist's dream and you could hear the sports editor shouting, "Hold the front page." Then there was the selection for the Ashes tour provoking what I felt to be a mountain of negativity, but whose gloomy prognostications turned out to be largely correct. Thirdly, England had won the second ODI against the West Indies, Stokes scoring 73, so that needed celebrating. The County Championship was obscured in a blizzard of chaff.

I tossed the paper aside, metaphorically that is, as I did not wish to be so reckless with my tablet, and tuned into the live stream at Taunton. The pitch was undergoing preparation and a groundsman could be seen taking a video of the pitch. Next thing I knew it was on Twitter, in a laudable act of transparency by Somerset – or self-defence.

As an aside, there were a lot of pictures of the Essex celebrations of their season. This prompted two thoughts. Firstly I hoped they put fizzy water in the champagne bottles, or at least the most subpar prosecco. Secondly, I was struck that the Essex captain, Ryan ten Doeschate, while taking part, wore a slightly detached air. It seemed worth noting that ten Doeschate's captaincy was an element in their success, using wiliness, authority and cricketing example to lead them to their triumph.

At Taunton weather conditions were fair *deo gratias*, and there was some local news in that Matthew Maynard had been sacked as the Somerset coach, a reminder that although Somerset looked to be winning the struggle to avoid the noose, they had not won any laurel crowns in the season: titles are not won by being sucked into a relegation battle. Football-club management requires that results rule okay, and cricket is not necessarily immune. However, unless you knew the politics behind it, it seemed an odd moment to announce the decision.

A decent crowd had turned up at Taunton. Somerset naturally

got their spin trio on, with Bess starting proceedings by completing the over interrupted by rain the day before. But the right-handed batsmen, Voges and Eskinazi, required Van der Merwe rather than Bess's use of foot marks to the left-handers. Van der Merwe is a left-armer spinning the ball away from the right-hander. Very soon he had Eskinazi squeezing the ball off the bat where it dropped just short of Trescothick, already on his knees. As on Day One Tresco needed to find his radar in this position so he then moved fractionally nearer. On the fourth ball of the over, the ball looped up off pad and bat in a catch that a standing Tresco would have taken. More arm-wrestling was needed, and on the fifth ball, Eskinazi was caught by the kneeling Tresco (below). There had been three edges in the over. The first was just short, although the commentators felt it was in fact a drop, the second spooned up, but the third was just right. Van der Merwe and Tresco had their man.

I speculated on whether Tresco had knee pads but he was in fact wearing wicket-keeper pads under his trousers. Was there some obscure rule of etiquette – not written in the Laws of Cricket, but still inviolable – that he could not wear them outside his trousers?

Next in was the left-handed Simpson so Bess was brought back on again, and Simpson took a boundary off a full toss. Then came Leach, exerting admirable control, with two slips and a silly mid-off. Voges was cleverly trying to disrupt Leach's rhythm and took two boundaries off him, but in the 29th over, to show that Middlesex's nerves were less than steely, Voges was almost run out when a direct hit on the stumps would have done for him. The next over Simpson hit Leach for six, and in preparation for the final showdown, the sun was coming up. Was there an extended battle in the offing? Middlesex were not going to make the runs required, and so their line had to be to make defence their best tactic against defeat, counter-intuitively spellbinding. Concentration by Voges and Simpson was the key to Middlesex's survival – and self-motivation to adopt this mode. Leach for his part had to find a similar discipline in preserving his accuracy. He had now bowled 18 overs for 30 runs and two wickets.

This particular battle was won by Leach when he made the crucial breakthrough in the 38th over. Voges, making an orthodox defensive push, was caught in the slips by Overton (below), who was proving no mean slip-catcher.

Simpson lbw
Leach

All the instincts of the new bat, Stirling, a stoutly Gatting-like figure in appearance, were stoutly attacking ones. While Simpson tried to apply stoutness to the defence of his wicket, Stirling reverse swept Bess so that the ball looped up just out of reach of leg slip. A few minutes later Simpson was caught on the crease by Leach and adjudged LBW (see sequence of images on previous page). Voges had scored 13 off 64 balls and Simpson 19 off 54. The Middlesex tale loomed.

With the left-hander gone, Van der Merwe came back on and promptly had Stirling caught by Overton in the slips. 80-7.

The radio was feeling the conclusion was foregone, and that if Somerset had not dropped chances it would be all over by now. The championship was ending on a high for them, and Abell's speech to the team in the Warwickshire game at the beginning of September was indeed proving to have been motivational.

For Middlesex only their quartet of bowlers – Harris, Finn, Murtagh and Patel – were left to face the music of Somerset's spin trio. I felt a pang for the tail-enders having to perform in the face of defeat, and possible relegation.

Harris was the first to go, and the wicket proved very strange to watch. The first image (see next page) shows Van der Merwe waiting to see the results of Harris's slog. The second image tells us of the batsman's downfall. He has been caught out of sight by Bartlett in the outfield and Van der Merwe is jubilant at the catch taken. Middlesex 94-8.

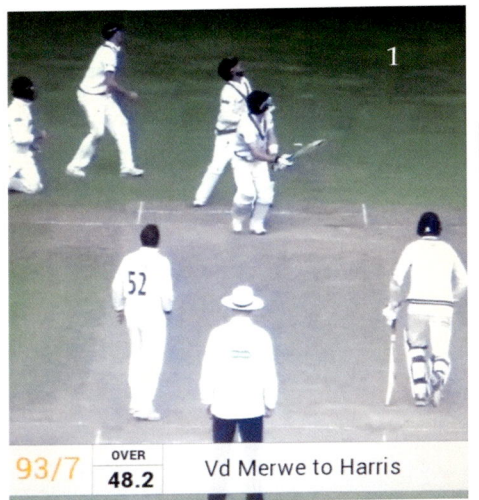

Finn and Murtagh were now at the crease. On the third ball of the 51st over Murtagh hoisted Van der Merwe for six, but next ball, coming down the pitch again, he was bowled (below). 101-9.

A new contest came into view: who would get their 5-for? Leach or Van der Merwe?

Leach's turn came first: dot (Finn forward defensive), dot (Finn sweeps and misses), dot (forward defensive), one run (Finn swings to leg), one run (Patel swings over mid-on), dot (Finn forward defensive).

Van der Merwe took the next over, possibly pleased that it was now his chance to get his fifth wicket: Patel would surely be his. I could see him taking a deep breath as he realised that getting too excited might impair his bowling. He spent the whole of the over putting his hands to his head: dot (ball spins past edge), dot (ball squirts to leg), dot (backward defence to silly mid-off), six! (Patel lands the ball on Gimblett Hill! One in the eye, ciderheads!), dot (ball beats Patel outside off stump), dot (forward defensive).

This was becoming a joust between the two spinners, with their fellow players going through the courtly motions and the spectators gazing and holding their breaths. I may only have been looking at a computer screen yet I was hypnotised.

Leach was more phlegmatic in his style. 54th over: four (Finn sweeps successfully and enjoyably), dot (forward defensive), dot (ditto), dot (ditto), wicket! (Finn LBW Leach - see below - for five off 29 balls). Finn stood at the crease reflecting on his LBW and, perhaps, the caprices of fortune, before finally and dejectedly departing.

Middlesex were 113 all out. Leach had bowled throughout both innings unchanged, and had his ninth wicket of the match for 111 runs, having bowled 266 dot balls out of his total of 309 balls in all. He abandoned facial severity to rejoice with his team-mates. The screen showed handshakes all round, with Ravi Patel, to his credit, very much among them. After all, he had had a good match. Elation for Somerset must have been the principal emotion, and then relief. Somerset had 147 points to Middlesex's 146, and for Middlesex the prospect was grim. However, not all was lost, since if Warwickshire could beat Hampshire and deny them any results points it would be Hampshire who would be relegated rather than Middlesex.

At 12:25 I went straight to the Warwickshire live stream to find Hampshire 59-1 with 200 required and 67 overs remaining, i.e. a rate of three runs an over, so victory for them was far from improbable. Play had been delayed by an hour because of overnight rain, which was good fortune for Hampshire and the first time in eight days that the weather was playing a deciding part. At Edgbaston the other Patel was in evidence: Jeetan, who had played 24 tests for New Zealand and taken 65 wickets, and who had been a firm fixture of the Warwickshire side since 2009. Having taken three wickets in the Hampshire first innings, he was surely motivated to improve that tally in their second. To Alsop, he was turning and bouncing the ball away from the bat. Warwickshire were not going to go down lightly – perhaps they could drag Hampshire with them?

The lunch break then ensued, and perhaps because I was still trying to calm down after the excitement at Taunton, I was ten minutes late in returning to my PC. My pulse was promptly set racing again, as no doubt were Middlesex pulses, when I found Hampshire were 72-3. Next Patel promptly had Bailey, the Hampshire captain, LBW for nought. So since the lunch break, three wickets had fallen for four runs, and Warwickshire must have scented their first victory of the season.

What should Hampshire do? Go for the win or play out a draw? James Vince, coming in at number four, had his own point to prove: his inclusion in the Ashes squad had elicited a certain amount of sceptical comment. It would be a good moment to swat away those pesky critics. 59 overs remained and 182 runs were needed for victory. Hampshire needed three runs an over, and Warwickshire a wicket every ten overs. As the battle continued, the sun came out and shadows lengthened to shoo away doubters about late-season cricket.

At 2:26 45 overs remained, with Warwickshire now needing a wicket every 7.5 overs. The Hampshire run rate, now down to 2.36 an over, seemed to indicate that their minds were inclining to a draw. The afternoon wore on. At 2:56 Warwickshire needed a wicket every six overs, but at tea around 3:10, Hampshire was still only four wickets down, albeit for only 113 runs. To anyone coming fresh to the game – and the end-of-season situation – proceedings would have felt somewhat in a rut, but to me it felt like a pinnacle of cricketing virtue: not just a four-day match was still in the balance, but a six-month season.

Things shifted in the second over after tea when Sidebottom, still bowling hard and intelligently, had Dawson caught at the wicket with the ball taking the edge of the bat. Dawson was out for nine, after 109 minutes and 94 balls of resistance. Hampshire's run requirement of 145 was barely relevant now. Ian Holland was the new bat and the radio discussed whether Vince should try to farm the strike. The commentators felt it was too early for him to do that while recognizing that he was key to the result: if he stayed, Hampshire would survive, but if he went, the risk of relegation would suddenly loom large.

Sidebottom was striving to seduce Vince into an error, and in the 67th over he got him to do so when Vince was caught by Tim Ambrose, the wicket-keeper, after 159 minutes at the crease and 124 balls. He only scored 30 runs but he had resisted waving away his wicket. Hampshire were now 124-6, so could Warwickshire bring home the victory that had eluded them at Headingley the week before? A mood of realism prevailed on the radio on the grounds that Patel's strike rate was "not good enough". He needed to take another wicket quickly and refuel his bowling.

At 4:18, with 20 overs remaining, only one other County Championship game was continuing, Worcestershire versus Durham in Division Two. We were into the last hour and a half of the season, a sentiment to induce a mellow melancholy.

At 4:22 Warwickshire brought back Christopher Wright to bowl and at 4:36, with 16 overs to go, a wicket was needed every four overs. That wicket would have to be forced.

With ten overs to go, Holland was taking on Patel, and Gareth

Berg the seamer. Warwickshire had six fielders round the bat, four on the leg, two on the off. To add to the general nerves, this was no time for the umpires to make an error, the radio commented. Patel however had perhaps done what he could, so with eight overs left Trott took the second new ball. Oliver Hannon-Dalby came on, but Warwickshire needed to speed things up because the lights had come on. One ball that was left by Berg sailed over the stumps; in the 83rd over Holland relieved pressure by hitting Sidebottom for four.

At 5:18, with five overs remaining, the crowd had gone quiet with some beginning to slip away, the pitch had gone dead with the ball not deviating, and, most ominously of all, the Middlesex Twitter feed had gone silent. Four or five fielders plus wicket-keeper crowded the bat, in "watery sunshine" as the radio put it, although at 4:50 the sun had been "beginning to disappear for the day" with the risk of poor light bringing proceedings to a glum end.

There was an interesting question of whether the conclusion this year was as exciting as that of 2016. Being involved in the moment I felt the answer was yes, but could a relegation scrap be as exciting as a title race? In 2016 three teams were in on the final session: Middlesex, Somerset and Yorkshire; here there were only two, Middlesex and Hampshire. Anyway sport is not for losers, surely? And yet . . . eight days, five teams battling to avoid relegation, the matter still not settled with half an hour to go.

With four wickets needed in four overs, normally the players would just shake hands on it. At 5:24 Holland and Berg's fifty-run partnership came up, and Sidebottom was looking decidedly weary. And then in the 86th over, the embers sparked again when Berg was bowled by Hannon-Dalby for 34, leaving Hampshire 14 balls to survive. Trott had turned back to Patel from whom a hat-trick would do nicely. In the 87th over, first slip missed a sharp chance off him. At 5:37, one over was left and a hat-trick from Hannon-Dalby needed: four, two, dot, dot. Suddenly it was three wickets left in two balls, a cricketing impossibility, so the players shook hands (see next page).

Give everyone back that lost hour at the beginning of play, I concluded.

A few minutes later, the staff were having the last word tidying up, and the unimaginable winter suddenly loomed (bottom image). Surely groundsmanship is Father Time's profession.

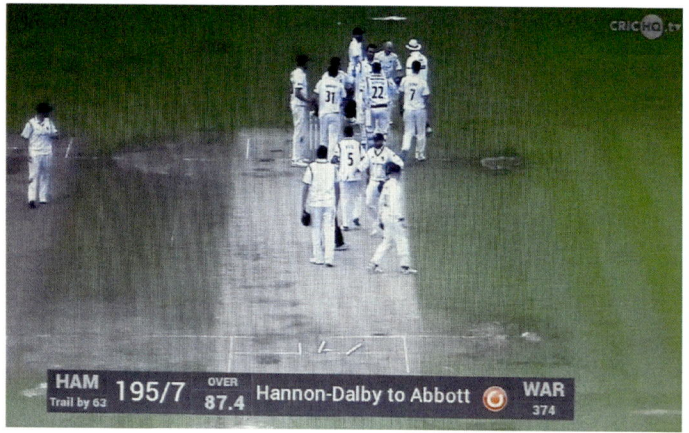

AFTERWORD

I know autumn has arrived when the fungi, which I have neither sown nor harvested, sprout and grow on the lawn. Their appearance feels predestined, provided I cherish them by neglect, and they will be there long after I have gone. They made their annual appearance the day after the Championship ended.

The County Championship has been in existence through various changes, tinkerings and restructurings since 1890, when it became officially so named, yet I feel no certainty that it will be around after I have gone. The forces of progress, in the process of dismembering it, may yet conclude by tearing it apart, limb from limb. While it exists however, the days after the last overs of the last game mark the end of summer and herald, like the fungi on the lawn, the beginning of autumn. Yet, counter-intuitive though it may seem, the ECB can take some credit for the excitements of the County Championship in 2017. Firstly, it is still allowed to exist. Secondly, the two-division structure brings real sporting tension into who takes the title, who gets the drop, who gets lifted up, and who does not. There is punditry now that the structure needs changing again, but to do that would risk creating something broken out of a structure that on the evidence of 2016 and 2017 is not broken. In any case, at least for the non-partisan spectator, and for the spectator who likes cricket because it is not football, the idea that two out of the top eight teams must go down – and they are likely to include teams with long and glorious histories – is intoxicating by comparison with the glacial dominance of the Premier League in football by a handful of teams.

Unlike football, there is only a modest financial hit from relegation to Division Two. More potent is the sense of honour that preservation in Division One upholds, and that relegation disturbs. Yet vicissitudes are a part of history and of our personal lives; to eliminate them in cricket would be a deceit.

Those eight days in September, as it happened, did produce that "bit of intensity" that Scyld Berry wished for at the outset, attractively understating the matter. Yet as well as the points battle, on display were good batting (for example, from Sangakkara, Stoneman, Hildreth, Browne – and several others), good bowling (Finn, Clarke, Jeetan Patel, Leach, Ravi Patel, and several others) and good catching: in their game against Lancashire, Middlesex took two blinders in the slips, and Trescothick makes up for loss of agility with a pair of hands that seem to snaffle nearly everything that comes his way, since he now has 534 catches in first-class cricket. There was something encouraging too in seeing a new generation of cricketers emerge, butterflies helped from the chrysalis by an older generation and spreading their wings. You sense continuity; you sense long-form cricket is not about to die through lack of good players coming forward; you sense these new players have a thirst to succeed.

Of the eight games on review, seven ended in a win or a defeat despite pessimists predicting that the weather was likely to spoil things. At some point it will happen, but not in 2017, nor in the climax to the 2016 season, nor in fact in 2015 when I watched Middlesex play Yorkshire at Lord's from 9 to 12 September in lovely sunshine. The one match that did end in a draw, Warwickshire v Hampshire, was as exciting as any other game, and it was a draw that ended in a very definite result since it ensured Hampshire stayed in Division One.

However, even the fairest rose can sicken. The few weeks following the end of the season were punctuated by two spats. Middlesex continued to fulminate about the pitch they had encountered at Taunton. One could see their point, but only up to a very limited point. The Somerset cricketers seemed to have set about the task with a greater intensity. Middlesex should have played another specialist spinner beside Patel and were unlucky that Ollie Rayner was injured. James Hildreth's unpanicked 109 was a significant difference between the two sides. Middlesex lost for cricketing reasons, but turned the pitch into an excuse. For the defeated team one may feel a touch of sympathy, but to reverse the result so that it was Somerset not Middlesex who were relegated felt out of the question.

At least lawyers were not involved in that affair, but they did come into play over 'arrowgate'. On 30 September, Middlesex requested a hearing with the ECB in an attempt to reverse their relegation by getting the two-point deduction rescinded. The Board could have rejected it on the grounds that there was no right of appeal but they conceded that there were in this case exceptional circumstances and that the matter would be looked at again. However, three weeks later Middlesex's appeal was rejected by the Board's Cricket Discipline Commission. Middlesex maturely agreed that it would not be in the interests of the game to take the matter any further – and Somerset were able finally to stand their lawyers down.

Although these shenanigans were not edifying, they were understandable. More sour was the knowledge that in their weather-ruined match with Yorkshire on 5 to 8 September, Middlesex declared their first innings on 272-8 with 3.1 overs left in the match, thus depriving Yorkshire of the chance to get two more wickets and garner a third bowling point. In a bunched-up table single points mattered, but this felt Jesuitical. Middlesex's plight seemed to be especially hedged around with 'what ifs?' What if arrowgate had not occurred? What if the Hampshire game at Uxbridge had not been so affected by the weather? What if they had drawn the Essex match in late June instead of succumbing to Harmer (9 for 95 in the second innings) with eight balls to go in the game? The sequence on the next page shows the tension of

Life is hard on tail-enders: Essex v Middlesex , 29 June, last wicket. Finn is at the crease when Harmer has his ninth scalp. As Essex cele-brate a famous victory, Finn, a still point in a blurry world (3), is left to rue what might have been.

those final balls as Essex have seven men round the bat plus the wicket-keeper and bowler. Was this the moment that Middlesex found themselves in the mire, or the moment when Essex put their hand on the Championship title? Perhaps both. What if Middlesex had turned more draws into wins, or, less abstractly, what if they had not fallen 17 runs short of a second batting point against Lancashire on 19 September? Finally, what if it had been Middlesex that had won the toss on Monday 25 September, and not Somerset?

And on the subject of 'what ifs?', in Division Two matters had concluded with Nottinghamshire on 222 points being promoted second to Worcestershire on 238 points. Northamptonshire on 217 points, despite a late charge, just missed out – but what if they had not messed up the over-rate and had five points deducted during the game against Nottinghamshire at the end of August?

Ill-feeling over these matters will simmer until erased by time and loss of memory, but in cricket that means a lot of time, nor is cricket tradition afflicted by amnesia. Forgiveness may not be forthcoming, so willed forgetfulness will have to be.

Middlesex were the losers, but cricket itself did not lose. This ill wind meant that Division Two teams would get to play at Lord's and who would deny them the pleasure in that? More hard-headedly, Middlesex's presence will allow players in Division Two to pit their skills against some fine players.

*

The melancholy of autumn gave way to a more marked discontent in the winter when England went down 4-0 to the Aussies in the Ashes, lugubriousness being briefly dispelled by the 4-1 victory to England in the ODIs. England had struggled against India the previous winter losing that Test series 4-0. County cricket was producing worthy candidates for England playing on home turf, but there is an awkward conundrum of how to adapt English skills to conditions abroad. Do Australian and Indian cricket fans now feel that playing England on tour is too easy, and therefore lose interest? Unless long-form cricket produces epic contests, will it remain under threat? There is a nexus, a chain between blast cricket, razzmatazz cricket, more popular cricket, and more lucrative cricket that is backing the long game into a corner. There are

not just batsmen evolving by leaps, heaves and 'scyvers' (will this neol-
ogism, to describe nutmegging a boundary from between one's legs,
stick, like 'googly' once did?), but bowlers too whose skills will allow
them to star in one-day (or shorter still) cricket, but whose bodies long-
form cricket risks wrecking. Players will commit to the short form, not
just for the money, but for the glamour. Cricket is naturally a global
game, but the Bash Leagues will only make it more so. Are the IPL auc-
tion and tournament conveying the same buzz as the World Economic
Forum at Davos: be there or be a nobody?

Blast cricket is for global citizens, a unifying force that brings
players and spectators together making them citizens of everywhere.
County cricket by contrast feels insufferably parochial, fodder only for
citizens of somewhere who are unable to join the elites. Thus it was that
in the night I would awake burdened with despair at the prospects for
long-form cricket, yet when I surfaced from sleep in the morning,
common-sense flooded back telling me that I was just being a Norwich
Hyperbolist. A healthy dose of optimism is in order. Some players will
continue to love playing slow cricket. Some players will evolve and
adapt to both slow and quick cricket so that the one need not exclude
the other. Surely it is true that things can change in order to stay the
same? Certainly, long-form cricket will need championing. At the
county level, at-the-ground support is small in number, even if high in
quality. But Will McPherson in *The Guardian* of 29 September, in re-
viewing the county cricket season, named his innovation of the year as
live streaming. "The championship is far too awkwardly timed to ever
be well-attended . . . but as social media, the interest in the various live
blogs, and the brilliant BBC radio commentaries show, there are a huge
number of folk remotely." So in-ground support is just the tip of an ice-
berg? I hope so. Certainly in my case following games online through
live streaming was an innovative highlight in 2017.

*

By the autumn those supporters had quietened down, although it must
be conceded that they were never very raucous in the first place. Slow
cricket has given way to slow thought. Concurrent with the cricket, the

104

news was full of the difficulties of the UK's negotiations in the exit from the EU. They hardly constitute a May 1940 moment (as *Dunkirk* and *The Darkest Hour*, the two Brexit films released over this period, reminded us) but they have produced a very downbeat mood. Superficially at least, the pessimists seem to have it, but reading Walton's 'The Compleat Angler' brought a different mood. Walton was 47 when the Battle of Edgehill took place, and 56 when the Roundheads chopped off the head of Charles I. As an unwavering Royalist, Walton must have experienced agony at the destruction of his certainties. How did he respond? By writing 'The Compleat Angler' as an amiable eulogy for the skills of fishing, for the pleasures of the countryside and for the virtues of the contemplative life. It is a retreat from the vice of despair, naive in its way, "lacking skill to deceive", and yet furnishing a profound comfort both to him and to his readers. Since its publication in 1653 it has hardly been out of print.

To remember those eight days in September is to cherish a pleasure of a similar order. While memory can play tricks, the human impulse to record word and image can ensure both that the memory is shared and that it can acquire a richer shade. To relive the facts in writing this book was a reminder that experiencing sporting success or defeat – triumph or disaster – is capable of producing an intense high or a numbing low, a rush of pleasure or a stab of pain, feelings which with the passage of time morph into something ripe yet without decay.

*

The last word must come from an unlikely source, the singer Joni Mitchell, in her song 'Big Yellow Taxi':

> "Don't it always seem to go
> that you don't know what you've got
> till it's gone."

FINAL POINTS TABLE DIVISION 1

Teams	Matches	Won	Lost	Drawn	Points
Essex	14	10	0	4	248
Lancashire	14	5	3	6	176
Surrey	14	2	2	10	163
Yorkshire	14	4	5	5	148
Hampshire	14	3	3	8	148
Somerset	14	4	6	4	147
Middlesex	14	3	4	7	146
Warwickshire	14	1	9	4	86

SUMMARY OF SCORES FOR THE EIGHT GAMES

Full scorecards can be found on Cricinfo and on the subscription service, www. cricketarchive.com.

19 to 22 September

Hampshire v Essex at Ageas Bowl:

- Hampshire 254 (Vince 60, G Bailey 89) and 76 (S Cook 11.4-6-18-5)

- Essex 76 (Abbott 11-7-20-6) and (following on) 362 (Lawrence 101, Bopara 57)

- Essex won by 108 runs; Hampshire 5 points (batting 2, bowling 3); Essex 19 (bowling 3)

Middlesex v Lancashire at Lord's:

- Middlesex 233 (Roland-Jones 53, Rayner 52; T Bailey 18-4-54-5) and 152 (Robson 58; T Bailey 16-6-44-5)

- Lancashire 165 and 184 (Finn 22.4-4-79-8)

- Middlesex won by 36 runs; Middlesex 20 points (batting 1, bowling 3); Lancashire 3 (bowling 3)

Surrey v Somerset at The Oval:

- Somerset 269 (Trescothick 65, S Davies 86; Clarke 18-2-55-7) and 306 (S Davies 52, Trego 68)

- Surrey 433 (Stoneman 51, Sangakkara 157, Pope 50, Clarke 50; Trego 28.4-5-67-5) and 146-4

- Surrey won by six wickets; Surrey 23 points (batting 4, bowling 3); Somerset 4 (batting 2, bowling 2)

Yorkshire v Warwickshire at Headingley:

- Warwickshire 219 (Bell 51, J Patel 100; Fisher 15.1-3-54-5) and 251 (Trott 59)

- Yorkshire 296 (Lyth 62) and 178-8 (Patel 28-17-50-6)

- Yorkshire won by two wickets; Yorkshire 21 points (batting 2, bowling 3); Warwickshire 4 (batting 1, bowling 3)

25 to 28 September

Essex v Yorkshire at County Ground, Chelmsford:

- Essex 227 (Harmer 64) and 334 (Browne 83, Lawrence 83, ten Doeschate 57, Harmer 58*)

- Yorkshire 111 and 74 (S Cook 8-0-20-5)

- Essex won by 376 runs; Essex 20 points (batting 1, bowling 3); Yorkshire 3 (bowling 3)

Lancashire v Surrey at Old Trafford:

- Surrey 201 (Curran 56*) and 242 (Stoneman 98; Livingstone 18-1-52-6)

- Lancashire 268 (A Davies 54, Croft 115) and 179-3 (Livingstone 69*)

- Lancashire won by 7 wickets; Lancashire 20 points (batting 2, bowling 2); Surrey 4 (batting 1, bowling 3)

Somerset v Middlesex at County Ground, Taunton:

- Somerset 236 (Byrom 56; R Patel 29.4-3-81-7) and 250 (Hildreth 109; R Patel 26-3-92-5)

- Middlesex 142 and 113 (Leach 26.5-12-57-5)

- Somerset won by 231 runs; Somerset 20 (batting 1, bowling 3); Middlesex 3 (bowling 3)

Warwickshire v Hampshire at Edgbaston:

- Warwickshire 188 (Sibley 92; Edwards 14-1-49-5) and 186 (Bell 77*)

- Hampshire 116 (G Bailey 55) and 195-7

- Match drawn; Warwickshire 8 (bowling 3); Hampshire 8 (bowling 3)

ABOUT THE AUTHOR

Tim Cawkwell was born in 1948 and lives in Norwich in the United Kingdom. He is the author of several books on film, travel and cricket:

- *The World Encyclopaedia of Film* (co-editor, 1972)
- *Film Past Film Future* (2011)
- *Temenos 2012*, a diary about the Temenos film festival in Greece in 2012
- *From Neuralgistan to the Elated kingdom: a personal journey inside Sicily* (2013)
- *Between Wee Free and Wi Fi: Scotland and the UK belong surely?* (2013)
- *The New Filmgoer's Guide to God* (2014)
- *A Tivoli Companion* (2015)
- *Cricket's Pure Pleasure: the story of an extraordinary match – Middlesex v. Yorkshire, September 2015* (2016)
- *The Tale of Two Terriers and the Somerset Cat - the scrap for cricket's County Championship 2016* (2017)
- *Belaboured* (2017)

In 2008 he launched his own website for writing about the cinema, www.timcawkwell.co.uk, later adding to it a Wordpress blog, www.cawkwell200.com. In 2013 he set up his own imprint, Sforzinda Books, as an outlet for his publishing. In 2018 he released *LIGHT YEARS: the film diaries of Tim Cawkwell 1968-87 / 2015-18* on DVD.

Compleat Cricket is his third cricket book after *Cricket's Pure Pleasure* and *The Tale of Two Terriers and the Somerset Cat* .